R31-45

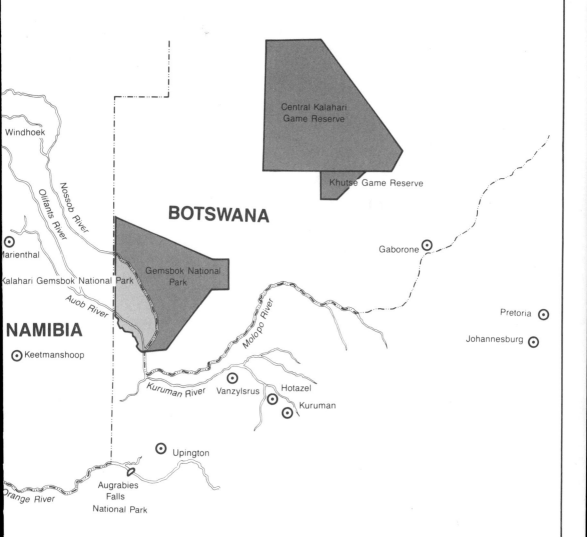

Windhoek

Central Kalahari
Game Reserve

Khutse Game Reserve

BOTSWANA

Nossob River

Olifants River

Marienthal

Gaborone

Kalahari Gemsbok National Park

Gemsbok National
Park

Auob River

Molopo River

Pretoria

Johannesburg

NAMIBIA

Keetmanshoop

Kuruman River   Vanzylsrus   Hotazel

Kuruman

Upington

Augrabies
Falls
National Park

Orange River

SOUTH AFRICA

Key

International Boundary

National Park/Game Reserve

River

Town

N

km

0   100

Guide to the

KALAHARI GEMSBOK

National Park

Guide to the

KALAHARI GEMSBOK

National Park

Gus Mills · Clem Haagner

SOUTHERN
BOOK PUBLISHERS

Dedicated to our wives,
Margie Mills and Peggy Haagner

ISBN 1 86812 206 9

First edition, first impression 1989

Published by
Southern Book Publishers (Pty) Ltd
PO Box 548, Bergvlei 2012
Johannesburg

Set in 11 on 12 pt Hanover
by Unifoto, Cape Town
Printed and bound by
CTP Book Printers, Cape

BK0269

Foreword

THE primary aim of this book is to help the tourist in getting the most out of his or her visit to the Kalahari Gemsbok National Park; however, it goes much beyond that. It is also an account of the natural history of the Kalahari. It is the story of the Kalahari's indigenous people, of its landscape and climate, of its animals and plants, written by two dedicated conservationists — one a scientist, the other a photographer, both masters in their own field. Like so many others the two authors have come under the spell of the desert and they write with feeling and warmth about the spirit and character of this unique ecosystem with its striking sand dunes and wide open spaces.

Survival is a major problem in a desert environment and the way the Bushman, the lion, the gemsbok and all the other mammals and feathered inhabitants overcome the harsh environmental conditions of the Kalahari by anatomical, physiological and behavioural mechanisms makes fascinating reading. Interwoven with the factual information are many anecdotes relating to the personal experiences of the two authors over the many years that they have scoured the vast expanses of the Kalahari desert.

One of the most outstanding features of the book is the photographs of the landscape and the plants and animals of the Kalahari. For the serious student of the fauna and flora there are complete checklists of the birds, mammals and the more conspicuous plants of the Kalahari Gemsbok National Park.

This book, with its wealth of information and beautiful illustrations, opens the door to one of the world's last wild places.

Prof. Fritz Eloff
Chairman National Parks Board

Acknowledgements

WE GRATEFULLY acknowledge the support of the National Parks Board of South Africa, the Botswana Department of Wildlife and National Parks, and all the staff in the Kalahari Gemsbok National Park — particularly the late warden, Stoffel le Riche, and his wife Judith, and the present warden and his wife, Elias and Doempie le Riche.

We are also most grateful to Sally Antrobus and Pam Blundell for help with writing the text, Denise Haagner and Margie Mills for typing the manuscript, and William Sepeng for much logistic support.

Research by the following people is quoted in the text: Brian Bertram, Koos Bothma, Thomas Butynski, Graham Child, Nicholas and Elsie Collias, Gerrie de Graaff, Fritz Eloff, Fay Goldie, Ray Huey, Hannes Kloppers, Mike Knight, Hans Kruuk, Otto Leistner, Richard Liversidge, Barry Lovegrove, David Macdonald, Gordon Maclean, Patti Moehlman, Jan Nel, Dick Parris, Eric Pianka, Colin Sapsford, Reay Smithers, Peter Steyn, Thea van Rensburg, Noel van Rooyen and Piet van Wyk.

Gus Mills
Clem Haagner

How to use this guide

THE Kalahari Gemsbok National Park is a long way from just about everywhere else, and it offers a game park experience distinctively different from that in other southern African parks.

This guide is aimed at providing the visitor with insights into the special behavioural, ecological and physiological adaptations of various wildlife species to life in the Kalahari — and the best ways of seeing these for oneself. It does not attempt to give detailed physical descriptions of all species occurring here (field guides can do this better), although there are checklists of species.

Instead, it emphasises wildlife activity patterns, interactions between species, and observations by people who have spent much time in the Kalahari. This is information not readily found elsewhere, and we hope it will enhance the experience of visitors to the park.

Contents

CHAPTER ONE

Introduction

KALAHARI is a word that grips the public imagination, and for good reason. It is a land of huge vistas, climatic extremes, and fascinating adaptations to harsh conditions. In recent years international interest has focused on the Bushmen of the Kalahari, perhaps because urbanised modern man hankers for the wisdoms and skills of a less frenetic age.

The Kalahari Gemsbok National Park of South Africa offers visitors the opportunity to see one of the last essentially intact ecosystems in Africa — as well as visiting a land where Bushmen once roamed. Add to that the open nature of the terrain, and you have fine wildlife viewing against a backdrop of high scenic drama.

History

THE first human inhabitants of the Kalahari were the Bushmen. They reached the area some 40 000 years ago and have survived there ever since, although they have now disappeared from the southern Kalahari where the park lies today. Their survival depended on wide practical knowledge of plants and animals, and their lives were dominated by the seasons, which required them to move about a great deal to take advantage of the variety of foods and water sources available in different regions.

The first black tribes to penetrate the northern Kalahari, some 2 000 years ago, were the Kgalagadi. They lived in comparative peace with the Bushmen and, in some instances, married Bushmen women. The Kgalagadi were eventually dislodged by Tswana people pressing in from the north and were driven to the southwest where they, like the Bushmen, became hunter-gatherers — but not before they had given the area the name it was to retain. Kalahari is derived from the Kgalagadi word Makgadikgadi, meaning salt pans.

By the middle of the nineteenth century the southern Kalahari was developing into a lawless frontier zone. The land was marginal for stockfarming and peripheral to the great struggles for possession of the southern African interior. Here the outriders of several tribes and nations — chiefly Tswanas, Hottentots and white men — met, hunted, and sometimes fought one another.

The first whites entering the area came to trade and the Kalahari people usually paid for their goods with livestock. One of the earliest traders was Christoffel le Riche, who settled near Rietfontein in what today is the Mier Coloured Settlement.

In 1891, the park area as well as a large zone to the south-west known then as Mierland, was annexed to British Bechuanaland. About ten years later, trouble arose across the border in German South-West Africa when the Hottentots rebelled against German colonial rule. Matters came to a head in a short, bloody engagement at Groot Kolk on the Nossob River, in today's Kalahari Gemsbok National Park.

Although well within British territory, German troops had set up a heliograph station at Groot Kolk for transmitting messages to German South-West Africa. A huge camelthorn tree served as an ideal lookout post. Despite this, at daybreak one morning, the camp was attacked by Hottentots; German soldiers were killed as they rose from their beds. The big camelthorn, stil bearing the horseshoes which the Germans had nailed to its trunk as a ladder, stood for many years marking the site of the massacre. Unfortunately, the tree was burnt down in 1976 by one of the large bush fires which occurred after exceptional rains earlier that year.

Shortly after the outbreak of the First World War (by which time the lands in question had been incorporated into the Union of South Africa), a series of boreholes was sunk along the Auob riverbed by the South African government. This was in anticipation of an invasion of German South-West Africa which did not materialise. But during that war, the need to determine the ground position of the 20th meridian — the South-West African border — led to the basic triangulation of the border areas.

After this the region was surveyed and a theoretical subdivision was made into "farms" of 12 000 and 15 000 morgen (10 200 and 12 800 hectares). The survey was carried out by a Scot, Roger *Malkop* Jackson, which explains how such names as Craig Lockhart, Dalkeith, Montrose, and Monro came to be given to some boreholes in the area. Jackson named some of the farms after towns in his mother country.

After the First World War, several white farmers settled as borehole caretakers along the Auob. They were allowed to stay rent-free as long as they kept the boreholes in good repair. In addition, six farms were allocated to whites. Similarly, a few farms were given out along the lower reaches of the Nossob. But life was tough. Neither the white farmers nor their Coloured counterparts, to whom the land was eventually given, could make anything but a marginal living.

To supplement their meagre resources, the local residents took to living off the veld by hunting and biltong hunters also began to invade from further afield in ever-increasing numbers. It was only in the more remote reaches of the upper Nossob River that the *status quo* was maintained, for here the Bushmen continued to live in harmony with animals and plants.

A park is born

TWO men grew particularly concerned about the carnage that was developing. They were Piet (Mof) de

Villiers, Inspector of Lands at Upington, and Willie Rossouw, a local farmer and son-in-law of pioneer Christoffel le Riche. They invited the then Minister of Lands in South Africa, their friend Piet Grobler, on a "hunting trip" and deliberately took him to an area denuded of game.

So concerned was the Minister by the lack of game that he began promoting the idea of a national park. Largely through his efforts, the area between the Nossob and the Auob rivers, reaching north to the South-West African boundary, was proclaimed on 31 July 1931 the Kalahari Gemsbok National Park. The boundaries of the park as we know them today were established in 1935, when the farms to the south of the Auob River were bought, as were one or two successful farms in the Nossob valley. This embraced an area of 9 600 sq km.

In 1938, a 40-km wide strip adjacent to the Nossob in Botswana was proclaimed a game reserve and placed under the management jurisdiction of the National Parks Board of South Africa, an arrangement which exists today. The Botswana reserve was greatly increased in 1972 to encompass an area of 26 600 sq km, with a maximum east-west distance from the Nossob of 170 km, and was designated the Gemsbok National Park.

Together, South Africa's Kalahari Gemsbok National and Botswana's Gemsbok National Park form one of the largest national park systems in the world. Covering a total of 36 000 sq km the combined area is substantially larger than the Kruger National Park. Surrounding the park in Botswana are additional large wildlife management areas, where controlled

hunting is allowed, but where man and his domestic animals have not been granted access. It is essential that the two national parks continue to be administered as a single unit. Any barrier to the movement of animals across the Nossob River will be the death-knell of the southern Kalahari ecosystem — the last more or less intact terrestrial ecosystem in southern Africa.

The first ranger appointed to the Kalahari Gemsbok National Park in 1931 was Johannes le Riche, son of pioneer Christoffel. He was paid the equivalent of R15 a month and was assisted by a Coloured constable, Gert Jannewarie. With only a few horses and a cart, the men undertook the formidable task of controlling an area of about 1 300 sq km. Merely to collect the mail from Askham, 100 km away, took about a week.

In spite of the difficulties, they made progress. It was not long before Johannes caught his first poacher, and the magistrate at Upington was sympathetic, realising the need to support the ranger. Accordingly, from then on, stiff penalties were imposed on poachers — equivalent to R30 for one antelope, which was a heavy fine in those days.

In 1934 disaster struck. Rain, so often a blessed event for the Kalahari, brought adversity to the newly established park. With the rains came malaria and Johannes le Riche and Gert Jannewarie both succumbed. A few days after his elder brother's death, Joep le Riche was asked to take over the running of the park. He agreed to do so until someone more suitable could be found. In the event, however, he remained for 36 years, until he retired in 1970. A new Coloured constable, Gert Mouton, was appointed, and the two men enjoyed a long and successful partnership.

Joep had married Cillie in 1934 and their sons, Stoffel and Elias, were both destined to play significant roles in the park. In 1970, Stoffel succeeded his father as warden and carried on until his untimely death ten years later. Since then the park has been run by his younger brother, Elias.

During a patrol in 1936, Joep le Riche met a band of 20 Bushmen near Seven Pans, in the centre of the Kalahari Gemsbok National Park. Piet Grobler had stipulated when the park was proclaimed that one of its functions would be to provide refuge for the Bushmen. It was thought to be in their best interests to move them to the park's headquarters, which were then at Gemsbokplein, in the Auob valley. There they could be looked after and would still be able to live their traditional way of life. Later, a second group of Bushmen from Union's End was also moved to Gemsbokplein.

In due course, however, it was thought necessary to withdraw their right to hunt in the national park, and as compensation they were given accommodation and provisions. By 1954, most of them had gradually drifted into Coloured settlements to the south, and, today, no Bushmen live in either of the national parks. The nearest area where Bushmen are now to be found in any numbers is in the huge Central Kalahari Game Reserve, some 350 km north-east of the Nossob.

A few Bushmen joined the park staff where they are greatly valued as trackers. Although they are "Westernised" and have lost many of their traditional ways and beliefs, two qualities they have not lost are their tracking skills and their amazing stamina. If required they will run 20 km or more across the dunes, even if they have not run for several months.

In search of treasure

FOR many years there were rumours that large diamond deposits existed along the Kalahari riverbeds and in some of the pans. Many of the early travellers came in search of these riches. However, the only diamond I know of from the Kalahari is a tiny rough stone which scientists from Pretoria University found in an owl pellet!

The best known search for diamonds in the Kalahari ended in tragedy. In 1958 a German geologist, Hans Schwabe, was passing through the park on his way to South-West Africa. At Twee Rivieren he had a long talk with Joep le Riche about whether there were diamonds in the area. The warden told him there were none. Instead of going up the Auob —the route to the border post — Schwabe went up the Nossob. When he got to Kwang, 170 km from Twee Rivieren, he started walking, leaving at his car a note which said: "No water for car, no water for myself, no food, follow this road. Monday 8:00 a.m. —H. Schwabe." A day later, the Botswana Police found the deserted car and told Joep le Riche. With his son Stoffel, then a game ranger at Mata Mata, Joep immediately set out to investigate.

When they reached the car, they found the radiator was still full. They followed Schwabe's spoor, which went off to the north. Some 20 km to the south was Rooikop windmill, which Schwabe must have passed shortly before stopping. It was clear that he was looking for something other than water. Along the tracks they saw that Schwabe had stopped to probe the ground with a hard instrument. They followed the spoor up a dry river and found more signs of prospecting. Towards evening, they saw far ahead a number of vultures in a dead tree. Ominously, the spoor began to show signs of unsteadiness. Finally, they found Schwabe's body; spotted hyaenas and vultures had already consumed most of it.

It was impossible to remove the body. So there, near Groot Brak, they buried Hans Schwabe, placing on his grave a cross made from two camel-thorn branches, his prospector's pick, tin canteen and empty water bottle. On the cross, Joep le Riche inscribed the epitaph: "Here lies Hans Schwabe. Died 22.10.58."

Apart from diamonds, the Kalahari has attracted adventurers searching for another elusive goal — the fabled "Lost City of the Kalahari". In 1885, an American named Gilarmi Farini, accompanied by his son, Lulu, claimed to have discovered the ruins of an ancient city. The location of the ruins, he said, was three days' journey by ox-wagon in a north to north-east direction from Kiki mountain. Most searchers believe this means a location of 60 to 80 km from the present-day Kijkij windmill.

Over the years many people have been excited by the prospect of finding the lost city. It would be an important archaeological discovery. A thorough investigation of the site might even unearth buried treasure. The prospects have intrigued many

searchers and, between 1960 and 1965, there were 13 expeditions, some of them well prepared and well organised. Probably the most extensive search was that made by a South African Air Force Dakota, which covered an area of 40 000 sq km.

Nearly all these expeditions were started because of the word of a Kalahari inhabitant who claimed to have knowledge of the lost city. These desert people either said they knew the location of the ruins, or knew someone else who knew. But none produced anything of value to the searchers, although locations were described at points as far apart as the Okavango and Nossob rivers.

It was not until the appearance in 1967 of A.J. Clement's book, *The Kalahari and its Lost City*, that an objective look was taken at the circumstances of Farini's original journey and "discovery". Farini's book, according to Clement, is riddled with so many contradictions and errors as to throw grave doubts on his claim. For example, by checking old passenger lists of the Union-Castle shipping line, Clement calculated that Farini had spent 175 days in South Africa. In order to have covered the distance that Farini claimed to have travelled on his journey through the Kalahari to Ngamiland, Clement calculated that Farini would have had to make 95 km a day, an impossibility in those days.

That is not all. Clement showed that there were discrepancies among the three accounts Farini left of the "ruins". His son, Lulu, who photographed nearly everything of note on the journey, failed to produce anything even vaguely convincing of the discovery. Farini has not been without supporters, who have said that since its discovery the lost city had been covered by shifting sands. The hard fact is that the sand dunes in this area have been stable for hundreds of years.

Another point that has been overlooked by most investigators is that, in his book, Farini implies that the ruins are of human origin. However, to the critical audiences he addressed at the Royal Geographical Society in London, he made no claim of any human agency. Clement concludes that what Farini probably found was a strange geological formation known as Eierdop Kopjies near the town of Rietfontein, in the south-west of the Mier Settlement.

Development of the park

DURING the past 30 years the National Parks Board has set out to encourage tourism in the Kalahari Gemsbok National Park. In the 1940s there were only three primitive rondavels at Twee Rivieren. These were humble beginnings. Today there are sophisticated and attractive air-conditioned accommodation, a swimming pool and a restaurant. In 1955, Mata Mata camp was built and, in 1966, Nossob camp was opened. While the number of visitors to the park in 1954 was 585, this had increased to a record 26 348 by 1987. During the early 1980s, a simple tourist camp and a small network of tracks were completed around Mabua Sehube, in the extreme east of the Gemsbok National Park in Botswana. While it is necessary to improve and expand tourist facilities, this must be done with caution and planning. The Kalahari's defence against over-development may be its most characteristic feature — lack of water.

A game-proof fence along the boundary of South-West Africa was completed in 1961, and a similar fence between the south-western boundary of the park and the Mier Coloured Settlement, was completed in 1963. These fences have restricted carnivores from crossing onto neighbouring farms. However the fences have not completely eliminated the problem as animals, including lions, sometimes dig their way under these "game-proof" barricades. In 1983 the fence between Mata Mata and Twee Rivieren was electrified and this has largely curbed these escapades.

Some of the border farmers have resorted to the sickening practice of throwing poisoned meat over the fence and setting gin-traps along it. The fences have to be patrolled regularly to keep animals and man from breaking the rules.

Current research

THE Kalahari Gemsbok National Park is a wonderful laboratory for the study of nature and natural processes. Not surprisingly it has attracted a number of researchers, both local and international, over the years. From modest beginnings the research facilities now include an aeroplane, sophisticated radio tracking equipment, a computer and accommodation for visiting scientists at Nossob camp.

During the twelve years that I was research officer in the park I concentrated on studying the ecology and behaviour of hyaenas; predator-prey relations; and the movement patterns of the ungulates in response to rainfall and the provision of water. Much of what I learned from these studies is recorded in this book.

In October 1983 a symposium on the Kalahari ecosystem was held in Pretoria at which nearly every person who had done research in the Kalahari Gemsbok National Park presented a paper. The proceedings from this symposium were published in a supplement to *Koedoe,* the scientific journal of the National Parks Board, number 27 in 1984.

The present research officer, Mike Knight, is continuing to follow the movement patterns of ungulates as well as carnivores by fitting radio collars to individuals and then tracking them from an aeroplane. This is an attempt to find out how large the southern Kalahari ecosystem is and how widely its larger inhabitants move. Gemsbok, wildebeest, hartebeest, springbok, eland, lions, leopards and cheetah have all been radio-tracked. Eland have been found to be the most mobile species. Mike has tracked some from Twee Rivieren right across to Mabua Sehube in Botswana. Two gemsbok cows moved from Kwai Pan in Botswana at the end of the dry season to Rooiputs in the Nossob River — a straight line trek of 130 km — and then back again after the first rains. Although the predators tend to be more sedentary, a radio-collared lion left the park and was shot after it supposedly killed two cattle in Botswana.

Mike is also studying the energy, food and water requirements of the ungulates. As part of these studies he and his wife, Annette, conducted a series of 24-hour watches at two boreholes of different water quality in the Nossob riverbed. One delivers sweet or potable water, the other salty or mineralised water. The animals showed a strong preference for the fresh waterhole, and at the mineralised waterhole they drank from the storage tank close to the outlet pipe if they could, in preference to the drinking trough provided. This is because the salts are far more concentrated in the drinking troughs where the water evaporates more quickly, leaving the salts behind, than in the large storage tanks. Spotted hyaenas which drink from Kousaunt have even learned to stand on their back legs, with their paws on the rim of the reservoir, in order to obtain less salty water.

Mike Knight is also continuing to monitor the Kousaunt spotted hyaena clan (see chapter 4). Through his work and mine all births, deaths, immigrants joining the clan and emigrants leaving it have now been documented for ten years. This has given a unique picture of the changes that have taken place in the clan over a long period, as well as the number of offspring produced by different females. This extended type of study has great value in that it contributes to our understanding of the way groups of long-lived carnivores are maintained and controlled.

In 1987 more than 30 scientists from institutions worldwide had projects registered in the Kalahari Gemsbok National Park. These included such diverse subjects as vegetation dynamics, the collecting of insects and parasites, chromosome analysis of large mammals, behavioural ecology of suricates, evolution of sociality in molerats, water and energy requirements of raptors, and man's impact on the environment.

One of the most detailed projects is the study by Dr. David Macdonald from Oxford University and his student Shaughn Doolan of the behavioural ecology of the suricate. These engaging creatures make beautiful study animals. They become totally relaxed in the presence of humans, which makes it possible to observe their behaviour in detail. They are highly social little carnivores and have a most interesting social system. The study has focused on the role of the individual in suricate society. Some individuals have been monitored for several years and the ways in which their social status and behaviour within the group has altered have been documented. This is important in understanding how sociality in carnivores evolved.

Colin Sapsford's study on the water and energy requirements of pygmy falcons has shown that these tiny raptors are specialist sand lizard hunters. Using sophisticated physiological techniques, Colin has shown that while the female plays the dominant role during incubation of the eggs, the male provides two-thirds of her energy requirements by feeding her at the nest. Once the eggs have hatched, however, both parents provide equally for the chicks. After fledging the young are almost totally dependent on their parents for food for another two months.

Unlike most birds that have been studied, pygmy falcons do not increase their energy expenditure during breeding. Instead their efficiency at foraging increases and they spend more time resting. Based on observations of 55 ringed birds it has been found that considerable local movements and migrations occur amongst pygmy falcons. However, the most successful breeders are those that have managed to occupy the same territory for several years.

It is hard to believe that a subterranean rodent like the Damara molerat could be a highly social animal. In fact the family to which this species belongs, the Bathyergidae, display the widest range of sociality of all mammals, from strictly solitary species to the naked molerats that live in colonies with a similar type of organisation to that of bees! Dr. Barry Lovegrove studied the Damara molerat in the Kalahari. He found that their food, in the form of large tubers, was clumped, and that they have to burrow, which takes up much energy, to obtain it. For these reasons he suggests Damara molerats have taken on a social existence and live in groups which cooperate in digging tunnels and share the food resources.

There is still so much to be learned. If one considers that over 100 doctoral theses have been written on a small European rodent called the woodmouse, it goes without saying that the Kalahari holds more secrets than we can ever imagine.

CHAPTER TWO

Landscape and vegetation

THE largest area of sand in the world is to be found in southern Africa. This vast expanse covers a staggering 1 630 000 sq km, stretching from slightly north of the equator to a southern extreme on the banks of the Orange River in South Africa. Its most westerly point lies in Angola and it reaches eastward some 1 500 km into Zimbabwe.

The sands originated from rocks lying within an immense basin formed in the south-west of this region. Over millions of years, even before the continents began to drift apart, the rocks were eroded to fill the basin with fine sand. In the most arid southern regions the minute sand grains are covered with natural ferric iron oxide, and the prevailing low rainfall has not been able to leach out the astonishing variety of colours to be found in this desert sand — colours ranging from vivid orange-reds to burnt amber, brown ochre to smoky pink. By the addition of moisture, iron oxide is reduced to white ferous oxide.

This then is the famous Kalahari. There are no lakes here, no flowing rivers. Temperatures are extreme: there are summer highs of over 40°C, and winter lows reach a bone-chilling –10°C. As in all desert areas there are few human inhabitants, so that vast tracts of land are unspoilt. But this frequently arid and often barren-looking terrain, which has a great beauty of its own, is home to thousands of plants and animals which survive and reproduce, century after century. Fascinating survival techniques abound in this hostile wilderness.

Pans, dunes and riverbeds

AS MENTIONED, the name Kalahari derives from the Kgalagadi people's word for salt pans. About 1 000 or more of these pans are scattered throughout the dunes, particularly to the north and east of Union's End. The pans, such as Moravet on the dune road between the Auob and the Nossob, break up the monotony of the dunes, and are a focal point for many wildlife species. The vegetation is similar to that found along the riverbeds (see below), except that there are very few trees. Like the riverbeds, the pans have important salt licks and seasonal waterholes which are created when rain washes minerals and fine soil particles from the sides of the pan and carries them to its lowest point.

When animals come to a pan we

may see the kind of interaction necessary to sustain the life of the pan. A herd of gemsbok comes to a salt lick, or a waterhole. They mill around, chasing one another and churning up the soil, which is later blown off by strong winds. A flock of ostriches may be next to visit the mineral lick. They have a dust bath and their feathers pick up the soil, carrying it away when they leave. In this way the depth of the pan is maintained, and it is ready for the next rains when run-off water, together with the minerals and soil particles, will flow into it once more.

If you fly over the southern Kalahari you will see that the sand deposits are arranged in a series of long, roughly parallel dunes which give a distinctive ripple effect. It is only outside the parks, in areas overgrazed by domestic animals, that the dunes are bare. Inside, they are covered with grass, bushes and trees. This soil is very sandy; if you dig through it you will not find changes in its colour or texture, and it tends to be compact along the dune valleys and loose on the crests. (If a vehicle gets stuck, it will almost always be on the crest of a dune!)

During recent geological time the Kalahari has experienced a succession of alternate dry and wet periods, each lasting thousands of years. This pattern still prevails. In phases of extreme dryness the vegetation vanishes. Winds redistribute the sands. Dunes, troughs and plains are formed. It is probable that the dunes assumed their present configuration and became "fixed" with the types of vegetation now found there only during the past 10 000 to 15 000 years.

In the wetter periods of the distant past, four rivers cut broad, flat floors several metres below the level of the plains, which tilt gently to the south. For the past 1 000 years, however, the Molopo River, which receives the other three rivers, has not run its full course, being blocked by dunes north of South Africa's largest river, the Orange.

Two of these rivers run through the national parks and are the main arteries of this giant ecosystem. The Nossob, an ancient river system, enters the Kalahari Gemsbok National Park at Union's End and meanders in a south-easterly direction through the park, virtually forming oxbows in places. For part of its length it forms the international boundary between South Africa and Botswana, and between the two parks. It finally meets the Auob valley five kilometres north of Twee Rivieren (Two Rivers), which is the headquarters of the Kalahari Gemsbok National Park, as well as its main tourist camp and southern entrance.

Between its steep banks the Auob follows a much more direct course. It enters the Kalahari Gemsbok National Park at Mata Mata, 115 km south of Union's End, proceeds towards the south-east and its confluence with the Nossob, which then runs southwards to join first the Kuruman and then the Molopo, about 50 km from Twee Rivieren.

These rivers are dry except for short periods during abnormally wet years; the Auob flows only about twice a decade (the last time it flowed through the park was in 1974) and the Nossob about twice a century (it last flowed in 1963, although in 1988 the Nossob ran briefly for a short distance within the park).

The riverbeds and some of the

pans contain large amounts of mica in the fine soil. Translucent mica sheets can give a riverbed a wet look even when it is bone dry. This, together with the frequent mirages seen in the area, can have a strange effect on the hot, dusty, and weary traveller.

Spectacular dust storms sometimes sweep up the fine river sand in huge clouds, darkening the sky and penetrating even closed windows. The insides of houses are covered in layers of fine dust, making living conditions distinctly unpleasant during these times.

Climate

THE aridity of the southern Kalahari is mainly due to its geographical position which is in the horse latitudes (25° – 35°S). These are high pressure zones which generally receive little rain. Most of the atmospheric moisture in the southern Kalahari comes from anti-cyclones moving in from the Indian Ocean, although the Drakensberg mountain range creates a rain shadow over the area forming a barrier to all but the deeper air currents. Sometimes rainfall is supplemented by a tongue of moist air coming down from Angola in the north-west.

The average annual rainfall is 200 mm in the extreme south-west of the Kalahari, increasing eastwards to 350 mm in the east of the Gemsbok National Park. An area receiving less than 255 mm of rain per year is usually considered a desert. The rainfall range, however, is wide. Taking extremes measured over the past 30 years, Mata Mata received only 56,5 mm in 1964, while Nossob had 660,1 mm in 1976. The distribution can also vary greatly in any one year, one area sometimes receiving three times more rain than another.

Most rain falls during awe-inspiring thunderstorms; usually there are about ten of these a year. In the morning there is a brisk north wind, and at about midday the first clouds begin to form on the horizon. An hour later massive cumulo-nimbus clouds, shaped like a gigantic anvil-head, have gathered. As the clouds form, the wind gets stronger. There is a distant rumble of thunder. The sky darkens. The winds begin to rage, whipping swirling dust from the riverbeds and making the sky even darker. There is a loud crash of thunder, and the first big drops of rain hit the ground, leaving small circles in the sand. A clean fresh smell rises from the wet sand. Soon all the circles disappear as the rain becomes solid, accompanied by more cracks of thunder.

Within half an hour a storm can pass and the sky can clear. The thunder rumbles off into the distance and a welcome freshness fills the air. Sheets of water in the riverbed and a big branch torn from a camel-thorn tree by the wind are testimony to the recent violence.

Usually, however, the Kalahari is cloudless. This causes extremes in temperature — high by day, low at night. Humidity is low, and this combined with high day-time temperatures creates high rates of evaporation. The annual evaporation from standing water is ten times greater than the average yearly rainfall. This means that naturally occurring water is available in the riverbeds and on the pans only for short periods in the rainy season. For the rest of the year there is none.

In the dunes, rain water does not form pools, but is absorbed into the porous ground. Loss of moisture from the ground and from vegetation — evapotranspiration — is very high during the day in arid regions. At night, however, rapid cooling takes place, even in summer, and the relative humidity rises, allowing plants to take in a good water supply from moisture in the air.

The extremes in air temperature are greatly accentuated at ground level. If the air temperature (measured in a Stevenson Screen which contains instruments for the purpose) is 40°C, the surface of the ground can be a sizzling 70°C; conversely the night-time ground temperature in winter can be 25°C lower than the air temperature.

The Kalahari does not experience the usual seasonal changes of spring, summer, autumn and winter. From October to April you can bank on it being hot week in, week out. There will be few days when the mercury does not rise above 30°C. From October to December little rain falls, but from January to April 70 per cent of the yearly rainfall can be expected. May to September are the cold, dry months, with little or no rain. Night temperatures are often below freezing, resulting in ground frosts.

Vegetation

THE southern Kalahari's status as a semi-desert is dependent primarily on its vegetation which is shrub savannah, or plains with very widely scattered trees. This growth ensures protection for the ground surface from excessive exposure to the sun; it binds the soil; and provides food for animals. Without this vegetation the area would quickly become a true desert.

Broadly speaking, plants are either perennials, which live for many years, or annuals, which germinate, grow, flower, seed and die in one year. Perennials are the backbone of the system, providing many animals with a stable supply of nutritious, high quality food in both the wet and dry seasons. The annuals can be regarded as an unreliable luxury, exploding into abundance when conditions are favourable, but remaining unseen during droughts. A list of the more conspicuous and common plants can be found at the back of the book.

Rain is the driving force behind the Kalahari ecosystem and when it falls the plants respond in a dramatic fashion. Within days of a heavy rain storm, the riverbeds take on a green tinge as plants emerge from their drought-evading dormancy. If the rains continue then this flush erupts into a spectacular panorama of greens, yellows, purples and whites. The large stands of yellow and green *duwweltjies* are a classic example of this phenomenon.

With the rains the animals begin to move into the riverbeds; first the springbok, then hartebeest and wildebeest and finally gemsbok. The valleys become a fascinating hive of activity. If, however, there are no follow-up rains, everything slowly sinks back into dormancy.

Annuals avoid the extremely dry conditions by completing their life cycles during the short rainy season, so they are forced to make more rapid use of the rains than the perennials. The annuals pass the long dry season with their seeds lying dormant in the soil. It is not only the brief rainy period which affects their growing season, but also the short time during which insects pollinate their flowers. Annuals often have large, gaudy flowers which attract insects and give the desert spectacular splashes of colour; but the display is short-lived since such flowers are expensive in terms of the abundant water they need. The seed crop annuals produce is extravagant — far greater than the minimum required for a species to survive a drought. However, these plants can afford to live flamboyantly because they utilise the water supply of the moment, providing for the future in their drought-resistant seeds. The surplus seeds also provide a bonus in the form of staple food for small rodents and birds.

Characteristic trees

THE most widespread of the Kalahari trees is the shepherd's tree or *witgat*. It is very common in the dunes and is the most important fodder tree in the area. Its leaves have a high protein content and are available throughout the year. The flowers are rich in nectar and are eagerly eaten by antelope, and the fruits are eaten by birds. Its roots may be roasted and ground to make a passable substitute for coffee, particularly if the nearest store is 150 km away!

Trees provide shelter for many animals during the blistering sum-

mer days. However, a high price is exacted from people and animals who take advantage of this shade. In the sand under trees in the dunes live hundreds of little tick-like creatures called sand tampans. These blood-suckers react to carbon dioxide exhaled by the hapless animals sheltering from the sun. Within minutes the tampans come popping out of the sand looking for a meal.

Their mouths conveniently exude an anaesthetic so their hosts are unaware of the bites, and do not rub them off. Having drunk their fill they then drop back into the sand to breed. Wild animals are apparently not worried by tampans, but people and domestic animals may develop painful, suppurating ulcers from the bites, and these can weaken them to the point of death.

In the riverbeds the most common trees are the majestic camelthorn or *kameeldoring*, some specimens growing to 15 m in height and, along the Auob only, the silvery-leafed grey camelthorn or *vaalkameeldoring*. Camelthorns can survive here because of their extensive root systems which penetrate many metres below the surface to find groundwater. Even when rivers are dry there remains some underground flow. Young camelthorns grow very slowly above ground, expending most of their energy in root growth until they have found an adequate water supply. Both types of camelthorn are common in the dunes, but there is not enough soil moisture for them to grow larger than bushes.

A third type of acacia present is the bastard umbrella thorn or *swartbas*, which grows along the sides of the upper Nossob and in the dunes to the east.

There is one interesting natural hybrid found in the upper Auob: a meld of the camelthorn and grey camelthorn, locally known as the *basterkameel*. It resembles the camelthorn, but has the greyer, silvery leaves and more curling pods of the grey camelthorn.

Only two other tree species are common in the southern Kalahari. One is the worm-bark false-thorn which grows in the northern areas, especially along the dunes close to the Nossob River. The leaves are known to be a remedy for parasitic worms, and the bark is an African cure for worms in both man and animals. The other is the silver cluster-leaf or *geelhout* which is sporadically distributed on the tops of dunes. There are also a few examples of the wild green-hair tree or *lemoendoring* and the smelly shepherd's tree, the *stink witgat*. These appear occasionally along the river banks in the extreme south of the park. One or two sweetthorn and buffalo-thorn trees make up the rest of the meagre tree list of the southern Kalahari.

Shrubs and grasses

ALONG the banks of the Auob and the lower Nossob, where there are no dunes flanking the riverbeds, the banks form exposed calcrete slopes, extending along the upper Nossob into wide plains. Two important plants growing here are the shrub known as *driedoring* — meaning three thorns — and the short Bushman grass or *kortbeenboesmangras*. With its feathery white plumes glistening in the early morning light, the Bushman grass provides an unusually delicate landscape in this often stark environment.

The dunes can best be described as a sea of grass, the dune crests being covered by a tall, thick grass known as dune reed or *duinriet*. It is an excellent sand binder and is responsible for stabilisation of the dunes. Interspersed with the grass are bushes and low trees, the most common being the blackthorn or *swarthaak*, candle acacia or *trassiebos* and velvet raisin or brandybush, also known as *bessiebos*. The latter produces a fruit which was, and probably still is, fermented and used by western Transvaal farmers to make a brandy called mampoer. Hottentots of the north-western Cape also used the fruit to make distilled spirits. As indicated, shrub forms of several of the trees also grow in the dunes.

When there has been abundant rain a striking annual grass appears called Kalahari grass or *suurgras*. It grows alongside the rivers and in the dunes in large stands, looking like fields of corn. Animals eat it when it is very young and tender, but as it matures it secretes a sticky, acid substance from the glandular hairs on the flowers and stalks. This acid causes open sores on the animals' tongues and they usually leave it alone. Once it has dried out, however, it makes good hay and can then be safely eaten. The abundance of this grass in one year and its total absence in another provide dramatic contrasts in this aspect of the landscape.

During the 1970s (1974 and 1976 in particular) the Kalahari had very good rains. The grasses in the riverbeds and dunes grew into a tall, thick mass. In the early summer of the following years lightning set the world alight and, thanks to the dense grass cover, large fires swept the Kalahari, burning down many of the camelthorn trees. The larger ones were particularly prone to being burnt down, most of them burning from the inside. Their blackened, hollow skeletons can still be seen today along sections of the Nossob River.

These fires were the most serious in living memory. However, they occur only rarely and most of the trees that succumbed were old and dying; it was easy for the fire to penetrate and ignite them. Their demise made way for new and more vigorous ones. On many of the surviving trees new growth occurred, illustrating the camelthorn's prodigious powers of recovery after fire. The burnt out trees have also provided shelter for seedlings and have benefitted small animals, providing them with an important new habitat. Lizards and geckos shelter under their bark, rodents live among the fallen branches, and birds nest in the treeholes. The camelthorn skeletons provide an eerie, stark beauty (and at sunset seem to take on the form of exactly the animal you are particularly anxious to see).

Strategies for survival

IF THE rains, when they come, are to help maintain the life of the ecosystem, then it is vital that seed dispersal should be efficient, and many Kalahari plants exhibit ingenious adaptations to accomplish this.

For instance, some seeds take advantage of strong winds (which blow regularly in August and September) by having wind dispersal aids such as "wings". Others, like the seeds of the Bushman grasses, are adapted to burying themselves by having a bullet-shaped structure at the end of a long plume. At its base two shorter feathery plumes branch out; these catch the wind, forcing the bullet head to twist into the sand.

Others, like the devil's claw or *kloudoring*, have fruits armed with long hooks which become entangled in animals' hair. Some grasses, like the annual *Setaria verticillata*, have seeds which stick to animals' coats, giving rise to their popular name of *klitsgras* or bristle burr grass. This grass grows only under camelthorn trees, where the seeds can easily latch on to animals that come to seek shade.

Large bushes and trees have deep and extensive root systems which strike down to the water table to get a constant supply of water. Trees and larger bushes produce their flowers and fruits seasonally, and in the dry period around September most of them drop their leaves and fruit. These provide excellent fare for the browsing springbok and gemsbok. It does not benefit plants to have their flowers, leaves and new shoots eaten. On the trees, most of these edible titbits are beyond the reach of foraging animals, but the bushes have to protect themselves with thorns and a proliferation of stems, putting all except the outermost flowers and shoots out of reach.

The seeds of these trees and bushes are another matter. They are encased in attractive packets of protein-rich pods which are shed when ripe. Ungulates eat the pods, and it appears that their digestive juices erode the glossy seed-coats, allowing water to penetrate and trigger germination, once the seeds have passed through the animals' digestive tracts.

Smaller shrubs with shallower roots obviously have problems in obtaining moisture. During dry times the *driedoring* stands stark and leafless, which helps the plant to cut down on its need for water. But within a week of the first serious rains this plant is ablaze with flowers, and the green leaves soon follow. If there is another dry spell the leaves are shed and, if it rains once more, the plant blossoms again. If the rains continue, there are no more flowers, but the green leaves remain. Springbok especially favour the leaves and flowers, but unlike the acacia, the *driedoring* (despite its name) has no sharp thorns to protect it. Perhaps its defence against heavy browsing lies in numbers: it usually occurs in high densities so that, proportionately, only a few leaves and flowers are eaten.

The perennial grasses resist drought by a different technique: surrender. They simply die back to ground level and wait for the rain. The relatively shallow roots, however have to protect themselves from excessive heat, so they have evolved long, dense hair-roots to which the sand adheres, forming a sand-sheath of 10 to 20 cm. This gives them some insulation against the furnace-like ground temperatures of up to 70°C.

Melons and cucumbers

PERHAPS the most amazing plants of the Kalahari are two wild fruits, the tsama melon and the gemsbok cucumber, which offer both food and water to insects, birds, rodents, antelope, carnivores and humans.

Both grow along the ground in the dunes, but the tsama is an annual, the cucumber a perennial. The tsama grows in irregular patches on a trailing stem like a pumpkin and it looks rather like a small, round watermelon. The cucumber has a metre-long, large, tuberous root plunging down into the sand. Its fruit is about a quarter of the size of a tsama, elliptical in shape and covered in smooth spines. It is pale green when growing, but as it ripens it turns a greenish-yellow colour.

The flesh of both fruits is low in calories, but rich in trace elements and vitamin C. As a moisture source they are indispensable — 90 to 95 per cent of their flesh is water. In addition, their seeds have good food value.

Both fruits are eaten by many Kalahari creatures. The *koringkriek* or armoured ground cricket, worms and various birds — ostriches, yellow-billed hornbills, glossy starlings and redeyed bulbuls, to name a few — eat the flesh. Rodents, including ground squirrels and porcupines, eat both flesh and seeds. Most of the antelope eat the flesh, and they also dig up and eat the extremely bitter roots of the cucumber. Even carnivores devour these fruits; brown hyaenas are very fond of them, and jackals and honey badgers sometimes eat them too.

Some animals eat the flesh of these fruits not only for moisture, but for nutritional value as well. For instance, even on nights when brown hyaenas have drunk water they will eat the fruit. They do not eat the protein- and fat-rich seeds, although some pips are taken in and pass out undamaged in their faeces. This may be an important means of dispersal for the seeds. Concealed in the faeces, the pips are protected from being eaten and destroyed by rodents. It is also possible that passage through the hyaena's digestive tract may assist germination.

These wild fruits are an important, sometimes vital, source of moisture for the Kalahari Bushmen, who sometimes use them as the sole source of water for many dry months. Usually they are collected by the women and cooked before they are eaten. The Bushmen dig a hole and light a fire inside it. When it is hot enough, they throw sand on it and place the melons on top of the sand. These are covered with more sand and hot ashes and left to cook overnight. In the morning they are ready to eat.

Sometimes the hollowed out fruit is used as a pot and pieces of meat are added to the flesh to make a stew. If the fruit is eaten raw, the melon is usually opened up at one end and the central part is cut out and eaten. The rest of the flesh is then mashed into a pulp with a stick and the sodden mass is then half-drunk, half-eaten. Whether modern man could survive for long on tsamas is debatable. Our fragile digestive systems would probably reject this unusual food.

The Bushmen also eat the gemsbok cucumber, sometimes raw, but generally cooked. It is simply placed in the hot ashes of a fire for several hours and turned from time to time. The pips of both fruits are fried or roasted, then crushed and eaten.

The perennial cucumber can be relied upon to produce a crop every year; its density varies from 15 to 60 fruits per hectare (100 m $\times$ 100 m) in different years. The fruits are susceptible to frost. After the first frosts, which are expected from May onwards, the cucumbers become burnt, then soften and quickly decompose. Tsamas, on the other hand, are frost-resistant; if they produce a good crop (a density of 125 or more per hectare) it will last into the following year. But in a dry year the tsama crop can fail completely.

Early one morning I discovered a somewhat unexpected use of the tsama melon. Walking through the dunes after a rain storm the evening before, I noticed that several dried out tsama shells held water. Looking more closely, it was clear from the spoor around them that small animals had visited them for a drink. As puddles cannot form in the dunes because the sand is so porous, this is a good way for these small creatures to obtain a drop of water; another example of the opportunism employed by the inhabitants of the Kalahari in order to survive in this vast, arid land.

CHAPTER THREE

Antelope: the importance of mobility

ALL animals face the primary tasks of finding enough food and water to sustain themselves and enable them to reproduce. Two major additional problems confront animals that live in hot, arid regions like the Kalahari. Firstly, the animals must be able to breathe and excrete waste products from their bodies without losing too much water. Second, they must be able to keep their body temperature below lethal limits and yet, as far as possible, avoid cooling themselves by water-expending panting, or sweating. Much of the behaviour of Kalahari animals, from the enormous eland to tiny rodents, has evolved to cope with these problems. Some, notably the gemsbok, have also evolved certain effective physiological mechanisms.

Finding moisture

TO PUT the whole matter in perspective, we must remember that all the animals which live in the Kalahari have done so for thousands of years without permanent water sources. It is only in the past fifty years or so since man has provided artificial water — in the form of bore-holes, in the Kalahari Gemsbok National Park — that some permanent water has been made available for them. Much of this water, particularly along the Nossob riverbed and out in the dunes, is highly mineralised or salty.

Carnivores can overcome the problem of obtaining water by drinking the blood of their prey and by extracting moisture from fresh meat. For animals that eat plants — herbivores — the problem is more intricate.

Because the Kalahari air normally cools down significantly at night, and relative humidity therefore increases, many plants are able to take up moisture at this time. By adjusting their time of feeding to night and early morning, antelope are able to take in food when its moisture content is highest. This provides them with the bulk of their water requirements. In addition, there are the water-storing plants, such as tsama melons and gemsbok cucumbers, to fall back on.

Most of the animals drink water when it is available and they make regular use of boreholes. Along the Auob riverbed between 1978 and 1982, several series of six adjacent windmills each were experimentally closed for a year at a time. In the first year, we closed down the six from Mata Mata southwards; in the second year, the six upstream from Twee Rivieren; in the third, the six in the mid-section of the river; and, in the final year, the top six again. Once a month I conducted game counts along the riverbed, noting carefully the exact position of each antelope. A computer was used to analyse the data.

We could find no effect on the movements of springbok as a result of closing the windmills; their attraction to a particular area was clearly influenced by other factors, such as the quality and quantity of food. Wildebeest, on the other hand, showed clear avoidance of the areas in which the windmills were closed, particularly during the hot dry times, and they tended to cluster around water, except during the rains.

Perhaps the most surprising results were obtained with the gemsbok. Although, on a broad scale, they were neither attracted to nor avoiding the areas where the windmills were closed, they were definitely attracted to the closed windmills themselves. This was not, as was suggested by some well-meaning observers, because they were pathetically waiting for us to re-open the windmills; rather, it was because the mineral content of the soil at the closed windmills was considerably higher than at other places along the Auob riverbed. The evaporated borehole waters at these windmills had left residual minerals behind.

In the Nossob, where the mineral content of the borehole waters differs widely, gemsbok show a marked preference for the highly mineralised boreholes, such as Melkvlei, Kaspersdraai and Grootbrak; and gemsbok are rarely seen at windmills where the water is sweet, such as at Rooiputs, Cubitje Quap and Union's End. It appears that gemsbok drink water in the Kalahari for the minerals they obtain rather than for moisture. Wildebeest, on the contrary, show a clear preference for the sweet windmills in the Nossob and avoid the very salty ones.

Temperature regulation in gemsbok

PHYSIOLOGICALLY, the gemsbok, or at least its close relative, the fringed-eared oryx of East Africa has been found to be remarkably well adapted to withstanding high temperatures, with little or no water available. One adaptation they have evolved is to allow their body temperature to fluctuate in response to environmental stress; this is known as adaptive heterothermy. When deprived of water and exposed to a temperature of 45°C, they do not sweat (and so lose water) to cool down their bodies; instead they allow their body temperature to rise to more than 45°C, for up to eight hours if necessary. The advantage of this is considerable because they save a significant amount of water. Moreover, once their body temperature rises above the outside temperature, heat will flow from the animal to the environment. Thus, as the air cools down at night, the animal can easily rid itself of excess heat.

It is a remarkable achievement for a mammal to survive at a body temperature of 45°C for such long periods. Most animals usually die if their body temperature reaches 42°C, as the high temperature damages their brains. The main reason the oryx is able to survive these incredible temperatures appears to be the cooling effect on the brain of a small network of blood vessels located immediately below the brain, called the carotid rete. Before the carotid artery, carrying blood from the heart to the head, enters the braincase, it breaks up into a fine network of vessels which are surrounded by veins of cooler blood returning from the nasal sinuses. This venous blood is cooler because, although the dehydrated oryx has not sweated at high temperatures, it has panted. In panting, cooler, moist air from the lungs passes through the nasal sinuses. The surface area of the sinuses, in arid-adapted animals, is larger than normal, thus providing maximum cooling for the returning blood.

Therefore, at the carotid rete, the venous blood returning from the nasal sinuses is several degrees cooler than the hot blood from the heart in the carotid artery. When the hot, carotid blood reaches the carotid rete, it is flowing in the opposite direction to the cool venous blood, providing ideal conditions for what is called counter-current heat exchange. Thus, the blood in the carotid artery is cooled by about 3°C immediately before it enters the brain, and the delicate tissues of the brain are apparently able to withstand this temperature.

Desert gazelles, such as the dorcas and Grant's gazelles also have a carotid rete and are, therefore, also able to withstand similarly high temperatures. So too, in all probability, is the closely related springbok — although the springbok has not yet been studied in this regard.

Feeding patterns and avoiding predators

ANTELOPE can either browse (eat leaves, fruits, roots, flowers of trees, bushes, shrubs and herbs) or they can graze (eat grass). Not only must the vegetation provide their basic food requirements, but it must also supply sufficient moisture to meet their water needs.

When green, the grasses along the riverbeds and around pans are superior in quality to grasses in the dunes, particularly as they are richer in essential minerals. Large concentrations of antelope occur along the riverbeds during and just after the rains. In the dry season, the leaves of shrubs, bushes and trees, and seed pods which fall to the ground like those of the camelthorn, are considerably more nutritious than grass.

A possible solution for antelope, therefore, is to graze in the wet season and browse in the dry season. But it is not that simple. Browse material tends to be widely scattered in the Kalahari and often occurs in small amounts at each site. A large antelope may experience difficulty in finding enough browse to live on. Even when browse material is found, a large antelope's mouth may make it difficult for the animal to feed easily on the small-sized pieces, such as leaves, which make up so much of this type of food.

On the other hand, there are several advantages to being a large animal in the Kalahari. Firstly, in general among related species of animals, the larger species have a lower metabolic rate than the smaller ones and, therefore, do not need such good quality food. Large mouths enable them to eat large amounts of the abundant, although low quality, dry dune grass. Second, larger animals are able to lose water more rapidly to keep cool than smaller animals, because they have proportionately greater water reserves. This is due to the lower ratio between surface area and volume of the larger animals. Third, larger animals are more mobile and thus better able to cover vast distances in search of food.

Every year since 1973 there have been two annual aerial surveys over a large part of the southern Kalahari — one in the wet season, and another towards the end of the dry season. The aim of these surveys is to gain an idea of the movement patterns of the antelope. In addition, there have been monthly ground counts from a vehicle along the riverbeds. These counts give a good representative picture, although not accurate totals, of the number of antelope in the vicinity of the riverbeds on a seasonal basis.

Of the seven common antelopes in the southern Kalahari, four can be considered large: eland, gemsbok, blue wildebeest and red hartebeest. But only the mighty eland — the bulls can reach 900 kg in weight —is predominantly a browser. Eland are, however, catholic feeders and will also, if necessary, take in large quantities of grass. Their extremely large size enables them to obtain browse material far higher up in trees and bushes than any other Kalahari browser can reach. Eland are reputed to use their horns with a twisting motion to break down large tree branches.

They are the most mobile of all the antelope, continually on the move looking for good foraging areas. At times, there are thousands in one particular area, at others hardly any eland at all. They rarely come into the riverbeds and, when they do, it is merely to cross from one side to the other. They usually live in large herds. However, because of the scattered nature of much of their food, these often break up into small groups spread out over a very large area.

Like the eland, the majestic gemsbok make the most of the food available by eating both browse and grass, although they are chiefly grazers. These 225-kg, masked Kalahari cavalrymen are more sedentary than eland, preferring the riverbeds at the end of the rainy season (April to May) when the grasses are mature. At this time, if there have been good rains, there may be a thousand or more gemsbok along the Nossob. As conditions dry out, they rapidly move out into the dune areas, visiting the riverbeds from time to time in search of minerals, which they either get through "braking" (eating the soil), or from drinking the highly mineralised water at many of the windmills. They generally occur in fairly small herds of five to twenty animals, although they sometimes form temporary herds of up to 150 animals.

The gambolling, 200-kg wildebeest and the high-stepping, 145-kg hartebeest are grazers. Many are found along the riverbeds in herds of fifty or more during the rains, when the grass is of high quality (although for some reason not known, few hartebeest go into the Auob). In good years almost 1 000 hartebeest will concentrate along the Nossob riverbed, but in dry years hardly any will come in. As the grasses along the riverbeds dry out, the hartebeest disappear from these valleys and disperse far and wide into the dunes and into areas where there is no water.

The wildebeest from the riverbeds, however, usually do not disperse as widely. The reason for this is that they are more dependent on water than are any of the other Kalahari antelopes — and artificially provided water is most common along the riverbeds. With this water, especially the sweet water, the wildebeest are able to survive for long periods on the poor quality grass. However, when conditions become really dry, they have to move out or die. During the droughts of the late 1970s and early 1980s, large numbers of wildebeest died along the riverbeds, their numbers reaching a low in May 1986 when less than 50 were counted along the Nossob and 16 along the Auob.

Only a small proportion of the southern Kalahari's wildebeest and hartebeest populations, however, come into the riverbeds. The hundreds of pans in the dunes also attract these grazers during the rains. Their dry season movements, like those of the eland, are still poorly understood; there is, certainly, no fixed pattern to these movements. One year they may concentrate in huge numbers over a relatively small area, while the next, they may gather in a completely different part or be thinly distributed over a vast expanse.

In August 1979, there were an estimated 90 000 wildebeest in the Kalahari Gemsbok National Park. When one flew over the area, it looked as if it had been invaded by hordes of large black ants. In the six preceding years and the five subsequent ones, there were never more than 1 500 wildebeest in the park at this time of the year. Then in the winter of 1985 another large-scale movement of wildebeest, this time accompanied by eland, was recorded into the Kalahari Gemsbok National Park and environs. Large numbers of these animals eventually died due to the excessive drought conditions.

Some springbok are always found along the riverbeds and on pans. When it is dry, these most graceful of the Kalahari's antelope are constantly on the move, looking for small patches of good quality food. When the food is green, they concentrate in large numbers, the resident population swelling with immigrants from afar. Springbok are particularly well suited to cropping very short veld and are the quickest to react to any green flush along the riverbeds. They are also efficient browsers, having small mouths which enable them to select small, high quality food items during the dry season. Obviously, the Kalahari agrees with springbok, as they grow bigger here than in most other areas. Rams weigh, on average, 45 kg and ewes 38 kg, almost a third larger than in the south of their range.

The diminutive, 10-kg steenbok are able to select with care small, high quality food items and are predominantly browsers. They live in pairs in restricted territories, which provide enough food for the pairs over the whole year. Because of their territorial base they are the most evenly distributed antelope in the Kalahari, preferring to live in the dunes.

Finally, there is the common or

TABLE 1
The maximum and minimum estimates of antelope in the Kalahari Gemsbok
National Park and the Gemsbok National Park to a distance of 30 km from
the Nossob River between 1974 and 1983. Counts were done in April and
September each year.

SPECIES	DATE	RIVER	DUNES	TOTAL
Maximum gemsbok	April 1983	748	18 093	18 841
Minimum gemsbok	Sept 1979	58	5 247	5 305
Maximum wildebeest	Sept 1979	1 265	170 840	172 105
Minimum wildebeest	Sept 1983	212	207	419
Maximum eland	Sept 1981	0	13 099	13 099
Minimum eland	April 1982	0	12	12
Maximum hartebeest	Sept 1981	859	17 967	18 826
Minimum hartebeest	Sept 1983	4	253	257
Maximum springbok	April 1974	7 359	5 625	12 984
Minimum springbok	Sept 1978	929	413	1 342

grey duiker, a medium-sized antelope averaging 20 kg. Like the springbok, the duiker here is about a third larger than elsewhere in its range. It is predominantly a browser. The duiker lives exclusively in the dunes, preferring areas where the cover is densest. It is not as common as the steenbok.

The harsh dry seasonal ecological conditions in the Kalahari have led to the evolution of a highly nomadic system for the larger antelopes. This is illustrated in Table 1 which gives estimates of the maximum and minimum totals of antelope in a large part of the southern Kalahari over a ten-year period. As aerial surveys and radio tracking continue, gradually we are beginning to understand more about their movement patterns. One thing that is becoming apparent is that during wet years the tree savannah areas to the north-east, with a high proportion of annual grasses, attract the grazers in the dry season. It is during dry years that the perennial grasslands, in the south-west, become important.

Except for steenbok and duiker, their feeding habits and dispersion patterns enable the Kalahari antelope to live in herds. This is useful in avoiding predation. There is safety in numbers, because there are more eyes and ears to detect predators and also because the more members there are in the herd, the less likely any individual is to be unlucky.

The larger species, such as eland and gemsbok, are often able to defend themselves and particularly their young against predators. When attacked by spotted hyaenas, eland come together in a circle-like laager, with their heads together and their backs towards the hyaenas. Whenever the hyaenas attempt to close in, the eland kick backwards with great force and like lightning. Gemsbok also kick, but more often face the hyaenas and charge with their lethal horns. Wildebeest and hartebeest rely on their great speed to escape predators. Springbok have several predator avoidance strategies (see p.26). Steenbok and duiker must rely on cover and concealing behaviour to lessen their chances of being caught, and they are also extremely nimble.

Breeding behaviour

S PRINGBOK, wildebeest and hartebeest males set up territories, particularly during the breeding season, in areas where there are concentrations of females. The large number of solitary males of these three species which are found so evenly spaced along the riverbeds are territorial males and not, as is often supposed, old males which have been kicked out of the herd.

When a herd of females comes into a male's territory, he actively tries to keep the females there and mates with any that are receptive. When the females leave his territory, he does not try to follow them and they become the property of his neighbour. Males which are not able to win a territory are subjected to a life of abstinence in bachelor herds.

The energy demands on a territorial male during the rut are severe. If he is not frantically trying to keep females in his territory, he is chasing off a herd of bachelors or defending his boundaries against a challenger. Little time remains for feeding and, consequently, the territorial male often rapidly loses condition. Eventually, his territory may be usurped by a stronger bachelor and he may

himself become a bachelor, or worse still, be caught by a predator.

Outside the breeding season, and even if conditions become so dry that the females move off to other areas, territorial males may stay on their territories, probably to make sure that when conditions improve and the females return and are ready to be mated, they are "in possession". They do, however, pay a price for the privilege of possessing a territory: being on their own makes them more vulnerable to predators. If conditions become too dry, the territorial system breaks down and the males forego their territories to search for better areas.

Wildebeest and hartebeest are seasonal breeders. Wildebeest drop most of their young in December and January; hartebeest, between September and November. Wildebeest drop their young at a time of the year when the chances are best of green grass being available for the vital first few months of their calves' lives, so that the cows are likely to be able to obtain sufficient calories to produce milk. If, however, the rains are late or fail, calf mortality is high as the cows cannot nurse their calves adequately. Hartebeest, on the other hand, drop their calves at what appears to be a bad time of the year for grazers in the Kalahari — usually before the rains.

Springbok also tend to drop their lambs together, but the time of lambing varies from year to year. It may be as early as September or as late as January. The factors which regulate this are not known, but it seems that in years of high rainfall they lamb earlier than in dry years. This leaves more time for rain in the dry years before the lambs are born. They also frequently have a smaller lambing peak in April, and odd lambs may be born in other months as well.

The little that we know about the gemsbok's social life suggests that gemsbok males also set up territories — but these are considerably larger than those of the species mentioned earlier, being up to 75 sq km in size. Gemsbok do not have a definite mating season (although more calves are dropped in the late winter), and are reasonably sedentary. Because of this, they maintain territories throughout the year. Non-territorial males do not live in bachelor herds, but join the females in the breeding herds.

Being less seasonal breeders, gemsbok do not, as it were, put all their eggs in one basket. They try to make sure that at least some of their young are born when conditions are favourable. But they pay the price for this because there are small gemsbok calves available for predators for a good part of the year. They do not swamp their predators with easy meals for a short period as do the other large antelope. This is to an extent counterbalanced by gemsbok being widely scattered, and so the calves are few and far between and difficult for the predators to find.

Eland males do not have territories. For such a mobile species, this system probably would not work. Instead, the herds are fully integrated, and a dominance system for mating rights is set up among the bulls. Eland calve throughout the year, with a peak between September and December. The calves are hidden for the first two weeks, after which they join nursery herds, which are always accompanied by a few adults.

Specialities of the springbok

NOT only are springbok able to regulate their lambing times, presumably in order to take advantage of varying conditions, but their rate of reproduction is also impressive. It is, as far as I am aware, higher than in any other antelope.

Nearly every adult female produces a lamb each year, no matter how poor the conditions. In other antelope, dry conditions severely depress the pregnancy rate. If conditions are especially good, six-month-old lambs may become pregnant and they will lamb at just more than one year of age, when they are not yet full-grown. Furthermore, within days of lambing, a female may fall pregnant again, and thus produce two lambs in a 13-month period. Other antelope can produce only one lamb a year.

The potential rate of increase in springbok, therefore, is nothing short of phenomenal. This is a useful adaptation to life in such a fickle environment. It means they are able to capitalise on favourable conditions extremely quickly. No wonder their numbers sometimes exploded in the almost unbelievable proportions recorded by naturalists who observed the famous springbok treks of the past century.

Even in the past 40 years, two such treks have been observed in the southern Kalahari. One afternoon in October 1946, warden Joep le Riche was patrolling the Nossob riverbed, just north of Kwang. He noticed a large cloud of dust ahead, and hurried off to investigate. Soon he encountered a mass of springbok moving slowly down the riverbed. He reported that the column was seven miles deep and estimated it to contain more than 15 000 animals.

Further up the Nossob, he encountered several more herds, some with more than 500 animals, all moving in the same direction. Three days later, when he returned to Twee Rivieren, he discovered that the main mass of springbok had passed out of the park into the farming areas, where they were shot down like nine-pins by the farmers, who were concerned about protecting their grazing. A few springbok were reported to have penetrated as far as the Orange River, about 250 km to the south.

The second trek was even larger than the first. In November 1950, a huge concentration of uncountable numbers of springbok crossed the Molopo River on a 300-km-broad front, from Botswana into the northern Cape districts of Gordonia, Kuruman and Vryburg. Again, most of the animals were shot by farmers along the international border.

The reasons for these astounding mass movements have long taxed the minds of scientists and laymen alike, and still no satisfactory explanation has been found. Fluctuations in climate and, consequently, quality of food, due both to drought and to excessive rains, are almost certainly implicated in some way. The animals seem to be moving either away from poor conditions, or towards exceptionally good areas. One thing is certain: the next springbok mass movement in the southern Kalahari, whenever it occurs, will be far better studied and documented than any previous one.

Newborn springbok lambs are vul-nerable to all kinds of predators, from martial eagles to lions. There are at least nine predators of springbok lambs in the Kalahari. Springbok have, however, evolved several ways of lessening this predation pressure.

One method is to concentrate the time and place of dropping their young. If conditions allow, springbok ewes about to give birth will gather on lambing grounds. Several hundred springbok may come together at this time if there is a suitable green flush to be found. Because of the territorial systems of most predators, limiting the area where lambing occurs ensures that fewer predators will be able to hunt the lambs. Moreover, limiting the time period of the lambing season ensures the predators are more or less swamped by the lambs. So many lambs are born that the predators can get only a certain proportion of them during their vulnerable early weeks.

The lambs themselves are well equipped to avoid predators. A very young lamb is left on its own to lie still, head on the ground and ears flat. The mother feeds several hundred metres away, returning only briefly to suckle her lamb periodically. Should a predator approach, the lamb will not move. I have, on occasions, seen a hyaena pass within a metre or two of a lamb without noticing it. Sometimes, though, the lambs are unlucky, and the predator walks right into a lamb.

The lambs grow very quickly. Within a month they are able to move almost as fast as the adults. By this time, the greatest danger is over. The lambs form large nursery herds which, again, may be an anti-predator strategy. A lamb in a group is far more difficult to single out.

The extraordinary gait of the springbok, known as *pronking*, may also have evolved as a device for escaping from predators. The legs are held rigid, the head lowered, and the large white, fluffy dorsal fan on the lower back is opened as the animal bounces along, as if on springs. This action is most often seen at first and last light, being performed by lambs as they gambol and chase each other around.

More seriously, it is performed by adults and lambs on the rapid approach of a predator. Wild dogs elicit the quickest response. Even a single wild dog, trotting 100 metres away, may alert a springbok to *pronking*. A pack of dogs, or even spotted hyaenas, running at a springbok herd will set the whole group going and this is a truly wonderful sight. Only when the predators get quite close do the springbok break into a full gallop.

Why do they do this? Surely if they ran away at full speed as soon as they saw a predator approaching, they would have a far better chance of escape. Perhaps the visual impact of a large number of springbok doing exactly the same thing throws predators into such confusion that they are unable to pick out and concentrate on any one particular individual, as they normally do. Alternatively, or additionally, the springbok *pronk* may have the effect of saying to predators: "Look, how high I can jump! That is because I am strong and fit! Don't waste your time and energy in trying to catch me!"

Pronking is also deceptive. The animals actually move far more quickly than it appears. They may even move faster when *pronking* than when galloping.

Occasional visitors

THERE are other large herbivores in the Kalahari, but they rarely come into the extreme southern parts. Occasionally, a small herd of kudu will be seen, and now and then a warthog appears.

The most unusual recent visitor was an impala ewe. She was first seen from the air by Elias le Riche a few kilometres north of Mata Mata in December 1977. She soon came into the Auob and, during 1978 and 1979, made the Auob her home. This ewe moved up and down the riverbed together with the springbok. At first, the springbok did not seem to know quite what she was and, if she approached too closely, would often try to chase her away. However, they soon got used to her and they would intermingle freely. In 1980, she moved into the Nossob and gradually moved up it, finally settling down in the area between Nossob camp and Kwang. She met her death in December 1982 when she was killed by a pack of wild dogs. She is not the only impala to have come so far south; every few years, someone in the area sees one. No impala, however, has stayed around for anything like the period this one did.

The intriguing question is: where do they come from? The nearest natural population of impala is in the Lobatsi area of eastern Botswana, about 500 km away. The only other possibility is that they may have escaped from nearby farms, but even this seems unlikely since I know of no farmers in the vicinity who have impala.

CHAPTER FOUR

Hyaenas: masters of the night

HYAENAS are often regarded with disdain. The 16th-century German naturalist Conrad Gesner reported: "They gorge themselves so gluttonously after finding a corpse that their bellies swell to become as taut as a drum. They then seek a narrow place between two trees or stones, force themselves through it and extrude the remains of their meal simultaneously at both ends"!

In a fairly recent article in a conservation magazine, words like freak, stupid, demented and ungainly were used to describe the spotted hyaena and the author stated that the hyaena had been despised and hated down the ages, this being only natural "because he is such a coward".

Why should statements like these be so often repeated about hyaenas in general and the spotted hyaena in particular? Are they true? Spotted hyaenas are indeed able to gorge themselves. At a single sitting one may consume a third of its body weight, which certainly causes it to bulge. They also have some strange anatomical features; the female's reproductive organs mimic those of the male. And they give vent to some very eerie and witch-like cackles.

But how can an animal that has one of the most highly developed social systems amongst carnivores be called stupid; one that can run at 50 km per hour for up to three kilometres be called ungainly; or one which is bold enough to chase lions into trees be called a coward?

Perhaps the main reason for this biased view of hyaenas is that so much of their activity takes place at night. It is seen only by those who are privileged to be able to go out at night and watch them.

The hyaenid family consists of four species: spotted, brown, and striped hyenas, and the aardwolf. All are found in the Kalahari except the striped hyaena, which is an inhabitant of north Africa and southern Asia, and is very similar in its habits to the brown hyaena.

Spotted hyaena society

THE spotted hyaena is the largest. Adult females weigh as much as 75 kg and the males about 60 kg. The female has a false scrotum and the clitoris is large and penis-like. It is, therefore, often very difficult to tell the sex of a hyaena and this explains why they were once thought to be hermaphrodites.

Spotted hyaenas are social animals living in clans, which in the Kalahari usually number about 10 to 15 animals of all ages. The adult female members are close relatives and dominant to the one or two immigrant males which usually join the clan. When two hyaenas from the same clan meet, they indulge in an involved meeting ceremony. They stand parallel and head-to-tail, each raising the back leg nearest to the other, and each erecting its sexual organ. They then mutually sniff and lick each other's organs. The cubs have proportionally large reproductive organs and are always keen to greet any of the other clan members in this way.

There is no sexual meaning to these meeting ceremonies. Rather they are used to cement the social ties among clan members. In greeting, the spotted hyaena presents its most vulnerable part to its partner's most lethal part — its teeth. This displays a high degree of trust between the greeting animals. Strangers never greet in this way.

The centre of clan activity is the den. This is generally a large hole in the ground, probably excavated by an aardvark and subsequently inhabited and enlarged by porcupines. Along the lower Nossob small caves in the calcrete also serve as dens. Spotted hyaenas are only temporary tenants and usually do not stay for more than about eight weeks at any one den. The main reason they move so frequently is that the dens soon become heavily infested with fleas. Hyaenas obviously provide ideal breeding conditions for fleas and their numbers at a hole quickly build up after the hyaenas have moved in. When the hyaenas are unable to stand the continual irritation any longer, they move on. Although porcupines usually move out when

hyaenas move in, sometimes the porcupines stay and the two species coinhabit the den, mutually ignoring each other and, one assumes, occupying different chambers underground.

The mouth of a den is often very large, but it quickly narrows into a tunnel about 50 cm wide and 35 cm high. Only the cubs can get down into these tunnels, which provide an ideal refuge for them during the long periods when the adults are away looking for food.

Nowhere are the social nature and friendly relationships of a spotted hyaena clan more evident than in the relaxed atmosphere of a den at sunrise or sunset. Some of the females will be lying around, suckling their cubs, while other cubs and some of the sub-adults are chasing and wrestling each other. Sometimes, they may crash into or "attack" one of the adults, which is lying down peacefully. An adult disturbed in this way may bare its teeth at the offenders, then quietly move away from the playground, showing considerably more tolerance to the restlessness of the young than people often do. The lower Nossob between Rooiputs and Melkvlei is a good place to look for spotted hyaena dens, and these hyaenas also sometimes den in the riverbed near Kaspersdraai and Bedinkt.

The members of a spotted hyaena clan do not spend all their time together. An individual may be on its own today; with two other members tomorrow; and in a group of ten the next day. Close relatives in a clan are more likely to move together than with more distantly related members and being in a group sometimes increases their efficiency at obtaining food. This is because the spotted hyaena is certainly not the original skulking scavenger, living off the remains of lion kills, but is itself a highly efficient and successful hunter of large mammals.

Scavenging does play a role in the spotted hyaenas' diet. But in the Kalahari, less than a third of their food is scavenged and the kills of other carnivores provide only a small proportion of these scavenged carcasses. Most of the carcasses are antelope that have died of starvation or disease. All hyaenas have a remarkably acute sense of smell and use it for locating carrion; they have very powerful jaws and teeth for crushing large bones, enabling them to extract the highly nutritious marrow, and are also able to digest bones. They are, therefore, well adapted to scavenging.

Even when spotted hyaenas scavenge from lion kills, they do not necessarily do so by patiently waiting while the lions eat their fill and then regally depart. The lions, in fact, may be persuaded to depart much sooner than they would like to, and in a manner hardly befitting their title of the king of beasts.

Clashes with lions

OLD Flat Ear, who is now dead, was the dominant female in 1980 of a clan of spotted hyaenas that live in the vicinity of Kousaunt. One evening I followed her from her den as she moved slowly through the dunes, stopping every few kilometres to lie down. After she had been going like this for about four hours, she started to move upwind at a much increased pace. Two kilometres further on she came upon a lioness lying next to a gemsbok carcass only partially eaten. The hyaena, pacing up and down for a few minutes, about 100 metres from the lioness, began to whoop in that most characteristic call of the African night. Six to nine whoops, in a bout, is the norm, each call lasting about three seconds. That night, however, Old Flat Ear whooped 19 times. Before she had finished there was an answer and, within a few moments, three other members of her clan — an adult female, adult male and half-grown male — appeared on the scene.

The lioness had been lying next to her gemsbok kill, seeming to pay little attention to what was going on. But now she got up, dragged the carcass further under a nearby tree and began eating. The three adult spotted hyaenas, after indulging in a prolonged meeting ceremony, closed ranks and, uttering all sorts of whoops, laughs, lows and grunts, advanced slowly towards the lioness.

She started growling and sat up to face the hyaenas. They were not impressed by this display and kept moving forward. When they were not more than five metres from the lioness, she made as if to charge the hyaenas, but checked herself. The hyaenas still kept coming forward and the lioness growled more loudly. When they were perhaps one metre away, the lioness's nerve broke and she bounded off, leaving the meal to her oppressors.

But it is not only when food is around that spotted hyaenas and lions clash. Spotted hyaenas seem to go out of their way to annoy and harrass lions. One night I was following six hyaenas. They had been moving slowly for several hours through the dunes, but when they came into the Nossob riverbed they began to lope. Earlier in the day, I had seen in this area a large herd of wildebeest and it seemed likely that the six hyaenas were approaching them.

After going at a steady 20 km per hour for three kilometres, the hyaenas suddenly darted off to one side and, in the moonlight, I could see a large animal fleeing from them. The chase was on, but I could not be sure what they were after. Five hundred metres further on I caught up with the hyaenas darting around a dead tree. I switched on the spotlight and there, clinging to the trunk of the tree with all her might, her ears flattened against her head, was a large lioness!

Four times I have seen lions take to trees to escape hyaenas and, on several occasions, I have also seen hyaenas mobbing lions, spending hours over it, preventing the lions from moving. Sometimes the shoe is on the other foot and the hyaenas do not have things their own way, particularly if there is an adult male in the lion group. Once, while I was watching four adult hyaenas and a large cub feeding on the remains of a springbok, a large black-maned lion came bounding up. The hyaenas scattered in all directions, but the cub was a little slow off the mark. The lion caught it and, with one shake, the cub was dead. The hyaenas came back and protested loudly, but kept their distance. The lion, after chasing the hyaenas a couple of times, came back to the dead cub, picked it up, shook it again, and then departed.

Why should there be so much animosity between spotted hyaenas and lions? The main reason is probably that they compete with each other for food. When lions come into an area which is being used by spotted hyaenas, it may be worthwhile for the hyaenas to make life as difficult as possible for the lions. Perhaps, then, the lions will soon move on.

Collective hunting

EVEN more exciting than watching spotted hyaenas mobbing lions is watching spotted hyaenas hunting. One evening I found five members of the Kousaunt clan near Kousaunt windmill. They obviously meant business as they started moving off down the river even before it was completely dark. They crossed an open plain in single file, five dark silhouettes strung out in a long line against the pale grass in the moonlight. After they had been travelling for nearly two hours, they suddenly changed direction and started to lope, moving into the wind, with their heads held up, noses in the air. They had smelt something. They were now moving at about 20 km per hour, ears pricked forward and eyes focused in front of them, bushy tails curled up over their backs — a sure sign that something was exciting them. They kept this up for nearly three kilometres, then, as we came over a small dune, a herd of about ten gemsbok appeared in front of us.

The hyaenas accelerated and the gemsbok scattered. Things were now moving so quickly that it was all I could do to keep driving behind one hyaena, who was racing across the veld at a good 40 km per hour. Using only my parking lights for fear of dazzling the gemsbok, I could make out another two hyaenas ahead, hard on the heels of one of the gemsbok. By now the chase had gone on for over a kilometre and it looked as though the gemsbok was pulling away from the hyaenas. The hunters, however, showed no signs of giving up and when the gemsbok swerved, the hyaenas cut the corner and started closing in. After a chase of two and a half kilometres, the gemsbok was obviously tiring and the hyaenas were right up to it.

The gemsbok tried to back up against a dead tree, but one hyaena grabbed it in the groin, at which a second hyaena rushed in and knocked the antelope down onto its side. I could now see that it was a young gemsbok, about one year old, weighing about 100 kg and with horns about 80 cm long. The gemsbok was trying to butt the hyaenas with its horns but, being on its side, had difficulty in using them effectively. By this time two other hyaenas had arrived, but they took little part in the actual killing, merely darting in and out of the others. Soon the hyaenas had pulled out the gemsbok's stomach and it was dead. The feast began.

Bolting down huge chunks of meat at a time, their faces quickly smeared with macabre masks of blood, the seven hyaenas polished off the best part of that gemsbok in an amazingly short time. After two and a half hours, all that was left was the head, some skin, and the larger bones. Anyone arriving on the scene now would probably say: "Look at the scavengers polishing off the remains of a lion kill."

Forty-three per cent of spotted hyaena kills are gemsbok under one year of age; 15 per cent are wilde-beest of all ages, and 10 per cent are adult gemsbok. Ostriches, springbok, eland — occasionally even adults — kudu, hartebeest, porcupines, steenbok, hares and springhares make up the rest. I have calculated that the 80 or so spotted hyaenas kill about 1 000 gemsbok calves per year in the southern Kalahari. They are, therefore, an important agent in controlling the gemsbok population.

Young animals are the spotted hyaenas' speciality. Whenever they encounter a herd of gemsbok they run into the herd, causing members to scatter. Any calves are quickly picked out and chased and, unless the calves can get back to the adults which can defend them, they are almost invariably run down by the hyaenas.

Adult gemsbok do not usually worry much about hyaenas. When gemsbok do encounter them, they will stand and face hyaenas, sometimes charging with their heads down. Occasionally, however, an adult gemsbok will run away from approaching hyaenas, whereupon the hyaenas will give chase. After several hundred metres, the gemsbok may back up against a tree or even go into a clump of bushes; or the hyaenas will give up the chase after two to three kilometres.

If a gemsbok does back up against a bush, the hyaenas will try a lot harder to get at it than if it had not run in the first place. However, they keep well away from the swinging, rapier-like horns of the gemsbok, and usually, the hyaenas eventually throw in the towel. If, however, the hyaenas manage to catch up with a gemsbok before it can reach the safety of a tree or bush and are able to pull it down onto its side, they will kill it. I once saw a gemsbok manage to get into a clump of bushes in the nick of time, having had its tail bitten off 20 metres away by a hyaena.

Why do some adult gemsbok confidently stand and face a pack of hyaenas whereas others turn tail? It probably depends mainly on the fitness of the gemsbok. A healthy individual knows it can ward off the hyaenas, whereas one not feeling at its best does not have this confidence and is put to flight. In this way, hyaenas are able to eliminate the less fit individuals which, in the long run, means a healthier gemsbok population.

Kalahari spotted hyaenas work hard for their living, particularly in the dry times when their prey are widely scattered. The average distance they cover each night is 26 km, with distances of more than 40 km not infrequent. The members of a clan use an area of up to 1 000 sq km. You can be sure this area is no larger than it needs to be to provide enough food for the members of the clan. It is not surprising, therefore, that spotted hyaena density in the Kalahari is low: there are only about 80 of them in the Kalahari Gemsbok National Park.

Brown hyaenas – solitary opportunists

THE more common Kalahari hyaena is the less well known, smaller brown hyaena. With their long dark cloaks, white collars and large pointed ears, brown hyaenas are handsome creatures. They weigh about 40 kg and are mainly inhabitants of the dry south-western regions of southern Africa. The Kalahari is the ideal habitat for brown hyaenas and they are the most common of the larger carnivores in the area. There are about 200 brown hyaenas in the park. But they are elusive creatures. The best way to find them is to drive slowly along one of the riverbeds at dusk or sunrise when they are most likely to be seen foraging. A lion kill or other dead animal is also worth visiting as early in the day as possible.

My earlier years in the Kalahari were mainly spent studying brown hyaenas with my wife, Margie. We attached radio-transmitting collars to certain brown hyaenas after catching them in a cage-trap and darting them. Each collar was tuned to a different frequency; thus by using a directional antenna attached to a receiver, we were able to locate individuals on a regular basis. Then, with the help of two green-glowing beta lights fitted to each radio collar, we were able to follow the hyaenas across the dunes and along the river valleys on their nightly foraging expeditions.

Brown hyaenas always forage alone, covering an average of 32 km and a maximum of 60 km a night in their search for food. They are predominantly scavengers. All kinds of vertebrate remains, particularly those from mammals, form the basis of their diet. These are supplemented by wild fruits, birds' eggs, insects such as beetles and termites, and, very occasionally small animals which the hyaena manages to kill.

The first night we ever followed a brown hyaena, it made a kill. The large cub had been plodding along for several hours, not having any luck in obtaining food, Suddenly, it lunged to one side and, at the mouth of a small hole, grabbed a striped polecat at the back of the head. The hyaena had chanced upon the polecat which had darted for the hole, but it was just too slow. Starting from the head, the hyaena then proceeded to eat the entire polecat.

We had to wait another three years before we saw our next brown hyaena kill, this time a korhaan, which was similarly snapped up as it was roosting on the ground. Other animals we saw brown hyaenas kill were springhares, a bat-eared fox and a springbok lamb, after chases varying from 50 to 1 000 metres.

Perhaps the most exciting night I spent with a brown hyaena was when an old female, called Cicely, discovered an unattended ostrich nest with no fewer than 26 eggs in it. She had obviously followed the ostrich's scent trail to the nest: for half an hour before reaching it, she had been walking slowly, nose to the ground, meandering back and forth. I do not know where the ostrich parents were, but they paid dearly for their negligence.

The rest of the night Cicely spent cleaning out the nest. She ate four eggs on the spot. The rest were picked up and carried off in different directions, never more than one kilometre from the nest, and then stored in a clump of tall grass or under a bush. The next night she recovered and ate three of the stored eggs. In two nights, she had eaten seven ostrich eggs — roughly equivalent to 170 chicken eggs.

She also had a supply of ostrich eggs from which to draw for the next few weeks. Evidently, brown hyaenas are not good at remembering the exact bush under which they have stored an egg, although they do remember the general area; several times, we watched hyaenas casting around at several bushes before eventually producing an ostrich egg from one of them. Neither, it seems, do brown hyaenas care if the eggs are bad. Once, as a hyaena bit open an egg, we heard a loud explosion and the smell that escaped was as bad as any stink bomb. The hyaena did not bat an eyelid and lapped up the entire contents of the egg.

Although nearly always seen alone, brown hyaenas are not the unsociable creatures they appear to be. Within each brown hyaena territory, the size of which is about 350 sq km, live several brown hyaenas, the actual number depending on the quality of food available. In a territory where the food consists mainly of small items, such as tsamas and scattered pieces of bone, the group size will be small, perhaps only a female and her latest litter of cubs, which take about 15 months to bring to independence. On the other hand, if there are large numbers of wildebeest dying because of drought and providing plenty of food for scavengers, as happened around Kwang in the late 1970s, there may be several adult brown hyaenas living in a territory. By the end of 1978, for example, the Kwang clan consisted of 14 members.

As with the spotted hyaena, most of the members of a brown hyaena group are relatives. All the adult females in the clan will breed, usually this is only one or two, although the younger ones may not do so as regularly as the older ones. Any member of the group which finds a piece of food suitable for the cubs to eat will usually carry it back to the den. A spectacular example of this was when we watched a brown hyaena carry almost half a springbok, weighing perhaps 15 kg, for ten kilometres — a prodigious effort of food-carrying. Food-carrying is shared equally by all the clan members and, in this respect, brown hyaenas differ markedly from spotted hyaenas, which do not carry food back to their young. Spotted hyaena cubs receive only mother's milk, until, at about nine months, they begin to join the adults on the hunt.

Apart from these group-living brown hyaenas, there are adult males which do not belong to any clan, but live a nomadic life ranging over a large area. When they come into a group territory, the members are friendly towards them, whereas clan members are not usually friendly towards their neighbours. So friendly are the clan members to nomadic males that the females allow these visitors to mate with them — it is, in fact, the nomadic males that do the mating and I have not seen a group-living male making sexual advances to females within or outside his clan.

We thus have the interesting situation among brown hyaenas that some males forego, at least for a few years, any opportunity to mate and, instead, stay at home and feed their mother's, sister's or cousin's cubs. Such situations are not nearly as rare among animals as was once believed. In jackals, foxes, mongooses, bee-eaters and sparrowweavers, to name a few, similar behaviour exists. These animals are exhibiting what biologists call kin selection; they are helping ensure the survival of youngsters which, although not their own offspring, are relatives. While not as good for passing on your genes as having your own offspring, such a

strategy does have benefits. An animal shares half of his genes with its offspring, a quarter with its sibling's offspring and an eighth with its cousin's.

In the case of the brown hyaena, going out and looking for a receptive female may be rather like looking for a needle in a haystack. Not only are females few and far between, because of the low density of brown hyaenas, but they usually come on heat only about once every 15 months. Also, even if a male finds a receptive female, he has no way of knowing whether he will be the only male to mate with her, as oestrous lasts several days and the male and female are not together all the time. Finally, it often happens that even after being mated, a female does not produce cubs.

Unlike spotted hyaenas, brown hyaenas are fairly silent animals. They have no whoop call, like the spotted hyaena's, which enables clan members to know where others are and to warn strange spotted hyaenas that the territory owners are around. The loudest sounds made by a brown hyaena are a loud growl and yell, uttered by the vanquished animal in the ritual territorial fights that occasionally occur between neighbours.

Communication by scent marking

THE brown hyaena does, however, have an elaborate form of indirect communication through the medium of scent marking. From time to time during foraging, a brown hyaena will come up to a grass stalk, walk over it, and extrude its large white anal gland. From the gland, it carefully deposits a creamy white blob on to the grass stalk and, about a centimetre above this, a thin black secretion, before moving on. The grass stalk will spring back into the upright position with the secretions adhering to it.

This scent marking behaviour, known as pasting, is a vital part of the brown hyaena's communications system. Each hyaena pastes with an average frequency of 2,6 times for every kilometre it moves. Considering that man, with his comparatively weak sense of smell, can still detect the scent from a hyaena pasting one month after deposition, to brown hyaenas the Kalahari must reek of hyaena pastings. A brown hyaena is rarely more than 500 m from a pasting.

Not all pastings however, smell the same to the hyaenas. They are able to distinguish the pastings of different individuals because the many chemical constituents making up a pasting occur in different proportions in each individual's paste. A brown hyaena encountering a pasting knows who has passed by and roughly how long ago. In this way, neighbours are able to recognise each other's territorial boundaries and members of the same group can perhaps avoid foraging in the same area at the same time, and thus avoid competing with each other for food.

Spotted hyaenas also paste in the same way but not nearly as often — only about 0,3 times per kilometre moved. Nor do they secrete such a complex paste. They mainly do it to mark territories. Unlike brown hyaenas, they do not have to avoid foraging at the same time in the same area as other members of their group; on the contrary, they often wish to forage in the same area. They do not, therefore, leave messages as to their whereabouts which another hyaena will recognise sometime later. Rather, they inform each other where they are through whooping, so that they can quickly come together for some co-operative venture.

Both hyaena species also demarcate their territories by regularly defaecating at certain areas called latrines. Latrines are distributed throughout the territory, although they occur at higher densities around boundaries. Because of the large amounts of bone they eat, hyaenas' droppings are large, white and conspicuous. Brown hyaena latrines are usually situated next to a tree, often a shepherd's tree, where spotted hyaena latrines may be atop a small dune, next to a dried out rain pool, or on the side of a road.

It is when there is a large carcass, with lots of meat on it, that brown hyaenas most frequently come together. Even then, however, the frenzied communal eating so characteristic of spotted hyaenas devouring a carcass does not occur. Usually, only one or two hyaenas feed at a time, the others patiently lying around waiting for them to finish. Often, a feeder will break off a piece and carry it away, either for consumption elsewhere, or to be stored in a clump of grass or under a bush. Immediately it moves off, one of the waiting hyaenas will go to the carcass. No individuals in the group consistently have access to a carcass over others, brown hyaenas feed on a first come first served basis. There is no dominance; they have a fairly egalitarian society.

Interactions between brown and spotted hyaenas

WHEN brown and spotted hyaenas meet, the result is usually an unpleasant experience for the brown hyaena. Should a brown hyaena be feeding on a carcass when a spotted hyaena arrives, the brown hyaena is certain to lose its meal.

One night I was following three spotted hyaenas which came upon a brown hyaena chewing a bone. The largest spotted hyaena, Olivia, the matriarch of the Kousaunt clan, rushed up to the brown hyaena, grabbed it by the side of the neck and started to pull it around roughly. The unfortunate brown hyaena, ears laid back in fear, growled and yelled in protest, trying desperately to shake itself free. The other two spotted hyaenas merely danced around the two struggling beasts like referees at a boxing match. Eventually the brown hyaena managed to shake free and ran off to the safety of a bush, against which it backed up. It was bleeding slightly and looked most dishevelled, but otherwise was unharmed. The spotted hyaenas for their part soon lost interest in the brown hyaena and helped themselves to the remaining bones.

Even when there is no food involved, meetings between brown and spotted hyaenas are normally unfriendly. The spotted hyaena will chase the brown hyaena, which will run off a short distance until it can back up against some cover. Although I have not seen spotted hyaenas hurt a brown hyaena badly, I once found a dead brown hyaena at Kaspersdraai and the surrounding spoor showed that it had been attacked and killed by spotted hyaenas. So these interactions do apparently sometimes escalate dramatically.

It is therefore strange that brown hyaenas, on occasions, invite such attacks. If a brown hyaena encounters spotted hyaenas, particularly if a spotted hyaena is on its own, the brown hyaena will often approach until it is chased away. Spotted hyaenas do not ordinarily press the attack home, but merely satisfy their curiosity. This attraction between these two species is also seen at other times; both will investigate each other's scent marks and will sometimes even place a scent mark over one left by the other species. This is unusual, as scent marks normally serve only as communication between members of the same species.

Brown hyaenas tend to avoid areas well frequented by spotted hyaenas. This avoidance is almost certainly due to the competition that exists between these two species for large carcasses, and the dominance and aggression of spotted hyaenas towards brown hyaenas.

In the Kalahari the few spotted hyaenas have little influence on brown hyaena numbers. In regions where spotted hyaenas are common, however, as in the Kruger National Park, I am sure that they have considerable influence on brown hyaena numbers and that this is the main reason why there are hardly any brown hyaenas in the Kruger Park. It is also interesting that Kruger spotted hyaenas often feed and forage like Kalahari brown hyaenas. Spotted hyaenas are probably the most important limiting factor in the distribution and numbers of the brown hyaena.

The diminutive aardwolf

THE third hyaena to inhabit the Kalahari is the diminutive 10-kg aardwolf, very different from the others. The aardwolf does not possess the formidable teeth of the hyaenas and, apart from two pairs of moderately large canines, it has only a few peg-like structures. It is probably the most specialised carnivore on earth, living almost exclusively on one species of soft-bodied termite of the genus *Trinervitermes*, and therefore does not need strong teeth.

While the aardwolf is similar in size to a jackal and is also called the *maanhaarjakkals* because of its impressive mane, chromosomal studies have shown that there is a close relationship between the aardwolf and hyaenas. There are also several anatomical and behavioural similarities between these species, notably the fact that the aardwolf uses pasting as a form of scent marking, a behaviour which is found only among hyaenas.

Aardwolves are rare in the Kalahari, probably because of the low rainfall and, consequently, the low density of their favourite termites. It is also possible that predators such as leopards, brown hyaenas and honey badgers keep the population down. Besides their rarity, aardwolves are nocturnal, and it is thus unlikely that park visitors will see one.

Previous page Brewing storm and dust devil along the Nossob riverbed.

Top The Auob riverbed and surrounding dunes from the air.

Right Hans Schwabe's grave at Groot Brak.

Top Fallen camelthorn pods sustain herbivores during times of food shortage.

Left Flowering *driedoring*. After the first rains they provide a nutritious and plentiful supply of food to browsing animals.

Below left Flowering catstail and wild sweetpea — conspicuous in some years, absent in others, depending on rainfall.

Following page A tsama patch — the fruits of these wonder plants of the Kalahari comprise over 90 per cent water.

Top Parallel dunes from the air — the dominant feature of the southern Kalahari landscape.

Left Flowering duwweltjies. These annual plants form dense stands after rains, particularly on disturbed areas.

Top left and below Kwang pan after good rains and Kwang pan during dry times from the air, showing the contrast between the two extremes.

Top A herd of gemsbok move through the Auob riverbed during the dry season. Gemsbok visit the riverbeds at this time mainly to obtain minerals.

Left Aftermath of drought — the dried out shell of a wildebeest. Wildebeest are more prone to drought than the other Kalahari antelope.

Top left Eland and wildebeest concentrations, 1979 dry season.

Left Hartebeest bulls clashing over a disputed territory.

Top right Springbok in a rain storm. This may herald the end of the dry season, or merely be an isolated incident.

Right A springbok herd on a red dune. Although they prefer the riverbeds and pans springbok do move through the dunes, especially in the dry season.

Previous page   Part of a massive concentration of wildebeest which entered the Kalahari Gemsbok National Park in the dry season of 1979.

Top   A steenbok browsing on camel-thorn leaves. Their small mouths enable them to select discrete, high quality food packages.

Right   Territorial wildebeest bulls size each other up.

Far right   A gemsbok herd in the Nossob riverbed during a period of good rains when they concentrate in this habitat.

Previous page A brown hyaena feeding on gemsbok remains. Brown hyaenas are mainly scavengers.

Top Spotted hyaenas cooling off in a water trough on a particularly hot day.

Right A brown hyaena female at the den with a cub. Brown hyaena females usually den alone.

Bottom right A spotted hyaena kills a young gemsbok calf, their principal prey in the southern Kalahari.

Far right A lion with porcupine quills stuck in his face and chest. Contrary to popular belief the quills will soon fall or be pulled out with no serious consequences to the animal.

Previous page   Set against the Kala-hari landscape, male lions look parti-cularly impressive.

Top   A female cheetah and her five large cubs approach a herd of wilde-beest, rather unusual prey for these cats.

Right   A lion rests in a tree — an un-usual occurrence for such large cats.

Top   A leopard rests in a camelthorn tree. Leopards are good tree climbers, frequently taking their prey into trees to escape competition from larger carnivores.

Left   Leopard portrait — perhaps the most beautiful of the cats.

Top   Four cheetah kill a springbok, their main prey in the Kalahari, particularly along the riverbeds.

Right   A lioness kills a wildebeest. Wildebeest and gemsbok are the lion's chief prey in the Kalahari.

Below right   An African wild cat, forefather of the domestic cat, in the Auob riverbed.

Far right   A suricate mounts guard atop a young camelthorn.

Top far left   A bat-eared fox. The large ears aid in the location of insects both above and under the ground.

Bottom far left   A yellow mongoose. These solitary little carnivores live mainly in the dunes.

Top   A black-backed jackal scavenges a springbok carcass.

Left   A honey badger or ratel prepares to climb a tree.

Following page   Three Cape fox pups — the only true foxes in southern Africa.

Far left   A giant eagle owl, largest of the Kalahari's owls. They can sometimes be found roosting during the day in large camelthorn trees near Twee Rivieren.

Top   A pale chanting goshawk feeds on a mole snake.

Left   A lappetfaced vulture dominates several whitebacked vultures.

Bottom left   The kori bustard — the heaviest flying bird on earth.

Top Male spotted sandgrouse wetting
their specially adapted breast feathers
to take water back to their chicks.

Right A male ostrich conducts the
broken-wing display in an attempt to
lure an intruder away from its chicks.

Below right A black korhaan. Their
striking colouration and raucous call
make them highly conspicuous birds in
the dunes.

Top A red-crested korhaan, equally as common but far less conspicuous than the black korhaan, at its nest.

Left Bateleur — one of the most conspicuous raptors in the Kalahari.

Below left A secretary bird kills a puff adder.

Top   A porcupine eating gemsbok cucumbers — important fruits for the moisture in their flesh and protein in their pips.

Above   A large bullfrog shortly after emerging from dry season dormancy.

Above left   A blueheaded agama male displays from a *driedoring* bush.

Left   Ground squirrels greet at their hole. Ground squirrels are social rodents often to be seen along the riverbeds.

CHAPTER FIVE

The cats

ONE night my assistant, Hermanus Jaeggers, and I slept at Gemsbokplein in the Auob River. It was a cold night, so we built a big fire and went to sleep under the stars close to it. During the night I heard a lion roaring some distance down the river. I realised he was moving upstream as a little later I heard him roar again, quite a bit closer.

At about one o'clock I woke up, and there in the starlight, not ten feet from the foot of my stretcher, was a huge lion looking at me with great interest. I felt decidedly uncomfortable as it was the first time I had ever looked up at a lion. It really brought home to me how big he was and how small I was in comparison. My first thought was: if he wanted to eat me, there was nothing in the world to stop him.

I sat up quickly, clapped my hands and in true South African fashion, yelled, "Voertsek!" For a split second I did not know which way he would go as he hesitated. Then he moved off into the darkness. The next instant he started roaring and moved away to continue his territorial tour. It was as if he was roaring in my ear; the whole world seemed to vibrate around me. It was one of the most thrilling moments of my life.

Until then, Hermanus had been sleeping peacefully next to me, totally unaware of the exciting time I had been having. As soon as the lion roared, however, he sat bolt upright and without saying a word, got up, put some more wood on the fire and went back to bed!

Six species of cat occur in the Kalahari, ranging in size from the tiny small spotted or black-footed cat, which weighs about 2 kg, to the mighty lion, with males weighing 185 kg or more. The other four felid species are leopard and cheetah, caracal, and the African wild cat, forefather of the domestic cat.

The majestic Kalahari lion

IN ANY national park in Africa, the lion is the animal most sought after by tourists. Despite being so indolent, particularly during the day, a large male lion with its head, neck and shoulders draped with a luxuriant black, tawny or silvery-blonde mane is indeed a marvellous sight. Set against the open landscape of the Kalahari, especially if it is atop a red dune, this sight adds dramatically to the semi-desert scene.

The Kalahari lion is often thought to be larger than other lions, but this is not so. Perhaps the openness of the habitat tends to exaggerate the apparent size of the animals. Neither is it true that the Kalahari lion is a separate subspecies. Over the past 200 years lions have been classified into almost two dozen subspecies, but most taxonomists now view all lions as belonging to the same species.

As with many higher vertebrates, lions are highly adaptable and are able to modify their behaviour under different environmental conditions. One of the ways this is done by the Kalahari lion has been shown by Professor Fritz Eloff. By following lion tracks in the sand, led by a Bushman tracker, Professor Eloff has found that Kalahari lions prey on small animals to a greater extent than their counterparts elsewhere in Africa.

Springhares, bat-eared foxes, steenbok and aardvark are all among the common food items of the Kalahari lions; but the animal that heads the list is the porcupine. About a quarter of all lion kills Professor Eloff found in the dunes were porcupines. He once followed the spoor of three sub-adult male lions for ten nights, during which time they killed one bat-eared fox and three porcupines. This reliance on small animals is obviously forced on the lions when the large antelope, their typical prey, are scarce.

A problem for lions and most other large carnivores in the Kalahari is the mobility and unpredictability of many of the large prey animals. Such patterns as have been detected in the movements of the antelope are mainly dependent on prevailing ecological conditions, especially rainfall. Probably because of the immobility

of their young, most of the lions do not follow the nomadic movements of antelope but are confined to territories. Each territory usually extending over more than 1 000 sq km, is inhabited by a number of lions, forming a pride, although the members of the pride seldom come together at the same time. There are nine or ten lion prides in the Kalahari Gemsbok National Park, which has a total lion population of about 150.

The nucleus of a lion pride is a number of adult females who are usually related to each other. In the Kalahari there are normally four to eight lionesses. Typically, only females which are born into a pride may stay with that pride as adults, and then only if there is enough food. Females expelled from their birth pride become nomadic. It is unlikely that these lions will breed successfully, unless, as sometimes happens, they are able to establish their own pride somewhere else. All males born into a pride leave it at about three years of age and they too become nomadic for a time. At this stage they are teenagers with scruffy manes, but during the next two years they develop into adults with full-sized manes.

Male coalitions

W HEN they have reached adulthood, male lions attempt to gain access to a pride by taking over a territory where males have left, or by evicting the male lions already there. This is often a violent affair and the losers may suffer death or serious injury. Male lions frequently form coalitions as their chances of gaining and maintaining a pride are then better than if they were on their own. All the males in a coalition, which in the Kalahari usually means two or three, are of equal status and there is little aggression between them.

Two well known males, called BE and BC, were found by Professor Eloff around Leijersdraai along the Nossob riverbed in January 1971, when they were young adults and had apparently just taken over the local pride. At the end of 1975, after about four years with the Leijersdraai pride, they left it (we are uncertain as to whether they were evicted or left of their own accord) and joined the neighbouring Kwang pride. Here they stayed for two and a half years until the middle of 1978, when they again changed prides and joined the Kaspersdraai group. Towards the end of 1981 they disappeared.

In December 1982 I found a very old and thin lion at Kaspersdraai and was surprised to see that it was old BC. About a month later he and BE were found at Kousaunt, some 55 km from Kaspersdraai, by Professor Eloff and warden Elias le Riche. BC was in a pitiful condition and it was decided to put him out of his misery. BE, too, was looking decidedly old and thin, but was not in quite such a bad way.

These two males must have been about 16 years old and had had a reproductive life of about ten years, compared with the four- to six-year reproductive life normally enjoyed by male lions in other areas. The difference may result from the low density of Kalahari lions relative to lions elsewhere, and the consequent reduction of competition among

males. The regular switching of prides by Kalahari lions may be an adaptation to reduce inbreeding: as a rule, a male's first daughters are ready to breed about four years after he has taken over a pride.

The coalition system among males does have its awkward moments, however. One night I found BC and BE moving across a plain just north of Kwang. After a few minutes, BC speeded up while BE followed at a slower pace. BC ran up to two jackals that had just killed a tiny springbok lamb and the jackals took to their heels as he approached. He immediately picked up the lamb, but before he could eat it, BE, who was considerably bigger than BC, was at him. BC spun round and ran off 200 metres, chased by BE, and then lay down on his brisket with the lamb underneath him and BE standing over him.

For the next 35 minutes these two huge cats fought over what to them was no more than an hors d'oeuvre. BE tried to pull the lamb away from BC with his front paws, while BC pushed BE away with all his might, claws poised over BE's nose and mouth. I thought they were going to kill each other. Then suddenly BC jumped free, the springbok still in his mouth, and within 30 seconds he had swallowed it! BE came running up to him and they clashed once more, rising on their hind legs and swiping and snarling at each other.

Then they parted and lay down some distance apart, licking their wounds — which, in spite of the apparent ferocity of their altercation, were remarkably slight. Not a drop of blood had been shed. After about five minutes, BE got up and moved over to BC, rubbed heads with him, and then rolled over next to him. BC got up and the two moved off together as if nothing had happened.

Cub survival

A FEATURE of lion existence everywhere is the surprisingly high death rate among the cubs; rarely will more than three out of ten cubs live for more than a year. Only one of 16 cubs Professor Eloff monitored in the Dankbaar area survived for more than 18 months. The main cause of death in cubs is starvation. Sometimes the mothers are forced to leave their cubs for many days in order to find food. They return to feed their cubs only when they themselves are satiated.

The situation is to an extent helped by the fact that lionesses will suckle each other's cubs. If one female is forced to stay away from her cubs longer than the others, they will care for the absent female's young. On the negative side, however, is the fact that, unlike hyaenas, lions do not leave their cubs in a safe hole, but under a bush. Thus, even if the cubs do not die of starvation, there is always the chance that a predator such as a hyaena — or, if they are very small, even a jackal — will kill them while they are left unattended.

Although starving cubs are a pitiful sight, there are good reasons not to interfere. Firstly, the adults may get lucky at last and be able to feed the cubs themselves. Obviously those cubs that survive the crisis will be the most resilient and, when they finally breed, they can be expected to produce tough offspring —

whereas if weaker cubs manage to survive through man's intervention, they may one day produce inferior lions. In other words, by taking this action we would interfere with natural selection and the survival of the fittest, the basis of evolution.

Second, the lion population in the Kalahari is in balance with its environment: it is a naturally regulated population. By intervening to allow cubs to survive today, wildlife managers would only be postponing the evil hour. When the cubs reached sub-adulthood they would be evicted from the pride to face an uncertain future as nomads, and would probably starve elsewhere. And if they did happen to breed, they would be contributing to an artificially high lion population, and their cubs would be even more likely to face starvation.

Moreover, what of the animal shot to provide food for starving lions? Why should the life of a wildebeest or gemsbok be sacrificed for that of a lion?

Wildlife managers have also periodically faced public pressure, when cubs are starving, at least to spare the animals' suffering and humanely destroy them. The problem here is to decide precisely when to take this action — for their hold on life is remarkable. In some instances, undoubtedly, we would kill a cub that would have survived and once again we would have interfered with natural selection.

Another cause of death of lion cubs is wilful killing by their own species — infanticide. Usually, after males have taken over a new pride they kill the cubs. This seemingly bizarre behaviour has been witnessed several times in the Kalahari and elsewhere.

One night I was sitting at Kwang windmill when I heard loud growling and snarling close by. I drove over to find a lioness from the Kwang pride with her two six-month-old cubs. Close by was an adult male who had recently come into the Kwang area after the previous pride males, BC and BE, had moved out. One of the cubs was badly injured; it could not walk on one front foot, one shoulder looked as if it had been dislocated and it had a large gash on its rump.

I believe that the male had just attacked it. The mother was obviously concerned and, although she appeared to want to move off, she kept coming back to her injured cub, because each time she moved away the male moved closer. After a time she moved over to her cub and tried to nudge it, at which the male moved even closer. The mother growled at the male and swished her tail and he lay down again. Eventually the male roared and moved off and half an hour later the mother and the fit cub followed his example, leaving the injured cub alone. They walked for three kilometres to join the male and some other members of the pride at a wildebeest kill.

In the morning the mother, along with her fit cub and another lioness from the pride, came back to the injured cub and they all moved off slowly to a large shady tree where they spent the day. Whether the cub died as a result of the injuries it had received or whether the male got hold of it again I do not know, but a week later I found the same lioness with three others, plus the male and only the fit cub. This cub had now also been mauled and had been bitten through the shoulders. Four days later I found the fresh remains of a lion cub at a brown hyaena den, near Kwang and, as I never saw the cub again, am sure that it was him, and that the male lion had eventually killed both of them.

The explanation for this infanticide is that a male who has newly joined a pride has no interest in giving protection to the cubs of other males. If he kills these youngsters, the females come into heat again and he can sire his own offspring. It is a selfish genetic imperative that drives males to actions which, on the face of it, seem detrimental to the survival of the species. The males do help their own cubs by sometimes allowing them to feed on a carcass, while preventing the lionesses from feeding.

Lionesses do not offer cubs too much maternal protection, because, being much smaller than the males, females run a real risk of getting injured themselves, and the chances are that their cubs will die of starvation in any event. Lion cubs are tiny in relation to their mothers and it costs a lioness little time and energy to produce young. Cubs can be replaced quickly and many times over in the course of a lifetime. If the cubs are older than about nine months, the females may be able to avoid conflict with the new males by temporarily leaving the territory until their cubs become independent.

With all this cub mortality, it may sound as though the Kalahari lion population is heading for extinction. This is not so. Because lions are long-lived animals with few enemies, once they are adults, their rate of replacement needs to be slow. In a pride with five females, there will probably only be a vacancy for another female once every two to three years.

Taking large prey

IN SPITE of the Kalahari lion's partiality for porcupines, it is as predators of large antelope that lions are best known. Kalahari gemsbok and wildebeest are the antelope most often killed by lions. These two antelope species are the chief prey of spotted hyaenas as well.

There is, however, a measure of ecological separation between lions and spotted hyaenas, as hyaenas mainly take gemsbok calves, whereas lions kill about three gemsbok adults to every calf. Similarly, lions kill considerably more adult wildebeest than do hyaenas. Springbok are the third most important antelope prey for lions, but make up only about one tenth of their kills.

Invincible as they seem, lions cannot kill at will, particularly in the Kalahari terrain. They often have to roam long distances to find prey and, even then, they are not assured of a kill. Because they have to stalk their prey and then charge when they are near enough, cover is of the utmost importance for successful hunting. Large areas of the Kalahari provide very little cover and most attempts at hunting are a failure.

Some animals are, however, more vulnerable to predators than others. For example, very young and old animals are generally slower and less alert than animals in their prime. These, we would expect, would be more likely to be caught by predators.

By examining the teeth of dead animals, it is possible to estimate their age. I compared the ages of wildebeest killed by lions with those of wildebeest shot for rations and scientific purposes; I found that in the lion sample there were considerably more old wildebeest than in the shot sample. This suggests that lions do in fact catch mainly older wildebeest. Similarly, lions kill far more gemsbok bulls than cows, even though there are equal numbers of cows and bulls in the gemsbok population. As most solitary gemsbok are bulls they are perhaps easier to catch than gemsbok protected by the multiple eyes and ears in a herd.

For the Kalahari lion, therefore, life is tough. In spite of its magnificent and regal appearance it has to work as hard to survive as any other organism in this hard and unrelenting environment.

Cheetah – the sprinter

A SPECTACULAR example of how natural selection has moulded an animal's body to its environment and way of life is found in the cheetah. Its long and powerful legs, its body shape, deep chest and small, streamlined head are all adapted for unexcelled speed. Its long tail acts as a counter-balance when twisting and turning. The cheetah is well known as the fastest mammal on earth. This marvellous sprinter is capable, over short distances, of speeds up to 95 km per hour. I once saw a cheetah charge a gemsbok calf, no mean sprinter itself, from 150 m and reach its prey within 400 m.

In order to attain this speed the cheetah uses tremendous amounts of energy in a very short burst. This causes a rapid rise in body temperature and if the hunter has not caught up with its prey after about 400 m at full speed, it has to abandon the hunt, probably because it cannot tolerate any further rise in body temperature.

The energy-consuming chase and kill often leave a cheetah completely exhausted. For several minutes afterwards it can do little but lie and pant heavily until it has regained enough strength to start eating. The cheetah I watched catching the gemsbok calf held the calf down for about a minute and then suddenly let it go. Perhaps the cat did not have enough energy left to dispatch this slightly larger than usual prey after the long sharp chase. The small streamlined head, so essential for speed, gives the cheetah the weakest jaws of predators of its size — it averages 40 kg in weight — and makes the killing of larger prey difficult.

Although Kalahari cheetah prey on a variety of animals — young gemsbok, wildebeest and hartebeest, steenbok and duiker, ostriches, hares, springhares and bat-eared foxes — springbok are their most important food. Cheetah predation on springbok, along the Auob riverbed, is one of the most significant predator-prey interactions in the Kalahari.

The Auob riverbed may be the best place in the world to observe cheetah hunting. The narrow riverbed tends to concentrate the springbok. Three or four female cheetah, together with their latest litters of cubs, as well as several males inhabit the area and its environs. A careful search along the Auob will often reveal at least one of these groups and, with some luck and more patience, it is likely that they will be seen hunting, as cheetah are predominantly day-time hunters.

During the springbok lambing season cheetah kill many lambs. But within a month the lambs can keep up with the adults and for the rest of the year cheetah kill mainly adult springbok. Nearly twice as many male as female springbok get caught, even though there are one and a half times as many females as males in the population. Springbok rams are clearly far more vulnerable to predation than are the ewes and, as with gemsbok, this is probably because while maintaining territories, the rams are so often on their own. The preponderance of adult females in the springbok population is at least partly due to this heavy predation pressure on the males.

By examining the teeth of dead springbok on the same basis as that described earlier for wildebeest, I again found that older springbok are far more likely to be caught by cheetah than are springbok in their prime. So, even with the cheetah's great speed, it cannot kill any springbok it chooses, but concentrates on the older and slower individuals.

Cheetah females have up to six cubs at a time. The males play no role in raising cubs, and cubs are dependent on their mother for about 18 months. As a single cheetah is perfectly capable of catching a springbok, a mother does not need the service of a male in helping to acquire food; he would, in fact, be competing with the mother and her cubs for food.

Females and cubs wander over large areas. One mother and her three cubs were seen at points 65 km apart along the Nossob valley, and another, with five cubs, at points 72 km apart. There does not appear to be any territoriality among female cheetah;

the ranges of different females overlap in an apparently random fashion.

Male cheetah often pair up or form a triumvirate and associate together for long periods in smaller home ranges than those of the females. Strange males are aggressively dealt with and it is not rare for males to kill each other. Two males I knew lived for a number of years around Kaspersdraai. These two obviously made a good hunting team since several times I found them feeding on almost adult-sized gemsbok, by far the largest prey I have known cheetah to catch.

Among the large carnivores, cheetah are at the bottom of the pecking order. Hunting by day helps them escape the attentions of their more nocturnal competitors such as lions, leopards and hyaenas, but even a brown hyaena can easily dislodge a cheetah from a kill.

One evening just after dark we were watching a female cheetah and her three small cubs feeding on a springbok. Suddenly a brown hyaena came running up to the carcass, his long coat flowing behind him like the academic gown of a schoolmaster late for class. The cheetah cubs retreated, but the mother came out to face the hyaena. The hyaena checked himself, turned around and retreated. His courage only failed him momentarily, for he soon turned back and charged the cheetah. They clashed, the cheetah swatted and growled, but the hyaena was not intimidated. The cheetah spun around and ran off after her cubs, leaving the brown hyaena with a bumper meal.

In contrast, jackals take no chances with cheetahs. When either species of hyaena is feeding, the jackals come right in to snatch a morsel from under the hyaena's nose. Even when lions are feeding, jackals come in quite close. However, when cheetah are feeding jackals rarely approach closer than 30 m, and are very wary. The jackals obviously respect the speed of the cheetah and will wait until the cheetah have completely finished eating and left the vicinity of the carcass before rushing in for what is left.

Cheetah never reach high densities in natural areas, competition from other carnivores probably being the main reason. The riverbeds of the Kalahari, with their large numbers of springbok and fairly low density of other carnivores, are as good a cheetah habitat as you will find anywhere.

The leopard's varied tastes

A COMMON nocturnal visitor to Nossob camp is a leopard. One night, I had left in my yard the remains of a springbok which I was using as bait to catch brown hyaenas. The next morning at sunrise, I was surprised to find the carcass in the large camelthorn tree outside the reception office! An examination of the spoor showed that a leopard, accompanied by a six-month-old cub, had been responsible and that a second cub had not managed to get over the fence.

Later that day I asked my assistant to lock the springbok carcass in my garden shed, as I did not want the leopard to steal it again. The next thing pandemonium broke out as I heard people shouting, "*Die tier, die tier!*" As the ranger was carrying the springbok into the shed, a baby leopard had jumped out from behind a pile of boxes, darted through the door and run off. Evidently, the cats had still been in the camp at sunrise when people started moving around. The mother had jumped back over the fence, but the cub, unable to do so, had taken refuge in the shed.

The problem was how to catch the cub. Although it was quite small and slow, it knew it was a leopard and we could not catch it with our bare hands. Eventually we threw a net over it. It became entangled in the net and when one of the rangers picked it up by the scruff of the neck, it lay motionless. We released it near the camp and two days later I saw the mother with both her cubs — and this time with her own springbok carcass.

This is typical of the leopard. Of all the large African carnivores, it is the last to disappear where man encroaches, often managing to live on our very doorstep without our knowing it. It is not surprising, therefore, that although the leopard is not uncommon in the Kalahari, it is the least often seen of the large cats.

One of the reasons for the leopard's success in many different areas is that it takes a very wide range of prey. Except for the brown hyaena, it has the most varied diet of all the Kalahari carnivores and has here been recorded preying on 20 species, ranging in size from mice to adult hartebeest. Unlike with the other predators, one or two species do not dominate the leopard's diet. Along the riverbeds, springbok are important, but in the dunes, where leopards seem to be plentiful, almost any victim may be chosen. Steenbok and duiker adults, hartebeest, eland and gemsbok calves, black-backed jackal,

bat-eared fox, Cape fox, aardwolf, wild cat, genet, porcupine, springhare, ground squirrel, aardvark and even ostrich have all been recorded as leopard kills, besides mice and hartebeest.

One night we were driving through the dunes when we found a very tame leopard who was not disturbed by the car or its lights. After following it for a short while, we saw it lie down in an open patch. A gerbil scurried by and, quick as lightning, the leopard pounced in exactly the same way as any house cat on similar prey. The leopard's paws hit the ground a fraction behind the gerbil which quickly darted into the safety of a hole. The leopard then moved over to a small thorn bush and pounced again. Suddenly a gerbil shot out of the bush and the leopard was after it, pouncing and swatting with its paws as it scurried hither and thither. After about 15 seconds, the leopard caught the gerbil in the middle of a bush. During the hour and a half that we followed the leopard, it caught another four gerbils, but missed three others.

The leopard epitomises the solitary cat. Males and females live in separate but overlapping territories and the female raises her cubs alone. Males, at about 60 kg, are considerably larger than females, which weigh about 40 kg. Territories of male leopards are larger than those of females, the territory of a male overlapping with those of several females.

Where its competitors are concerned, the leopard dominates only the cheetah. A leopard is no match for a lion, and spotted hyaenas regularly get the upper hand against them; leopards usually flee into trees if they are threatened by spotted hyaenas. With brown hyaenas the balance is more equal, but in my experience, the scales usually tip in favour of the hyaenas.

Once, for example, I had immobilised a brown hyaena in order to obtain some anal gland secretions for analysis. As the hyaena was recovering from the drug, a large male leopard came to the bait. I was concerned about what might happen to the hyaena in its semi-drugged state should the leopard decide to attack it. I need not have worried — about half an hour after getting up, the hyaena, still a little groggy, ran over to the leopard with its mane raised, at which the leopard turned tail and left the scene.

By taking their food into trees, leopards have evolved a master strategy for keeping the food from being plundered. The strength required to hoist a 40 kg springbok carcass several metres up a tree is staggering. On several occasions I have seen hyaenas of both species come to a tree in which a leopard has placed a juicy carcass. The hyaenas stand under the tree, staring up and sniffing at the food for several minutes. Sometimes they will even try to get at the food by stretching up the trunk on their hind legs. They move off a short distance, then come back; but they are wasting their time and eventually they move off and are seen no more. At best, the hyaenas will pick up a few scraps which have fallen off the carcass. The same goes for jackals, and vultures cannot locate a carcass hidden by the leaves of a tree. The only time I knew a leopard to lose its kill from a tree was when a young lion climbed the tree and removed the carcass.

Caracal – little, but fierce

LARGEST of the smaller cats in the Kalahari is the caracal, sometimes called the African lynx. Weighing about 15 kg, this handsome cat has brick-red colouring with long black tassels at the ends of its pointed ears. Like the lynx of Europe and North America (although it is not closely related to them), the caracal has a very short tail. Like most cats, the caracal is solitary.

It is capable of killing prey as large as adult springbok but lives mainly on smaller fare such as steenbok, duikers, springhares and small rodents, as well as ground nesting birds. I twice found a caracal feeding on a black-backed jackal and have twice seen them feeding on wild cats, which is perhaps testimony to the fact that Kalahari carnivores cannot afford to be too discriminating in their diet.

Once I found a caracal feeding on the fresh carcass of an adult male ostrich. The ostrich had two small holes in the back of its head which appeared to have been caused by the caracal's canines. There was no indication of a struggle which, if the caracal had killed the ostrich, there must surely have been, and in any event, how did the caracal manage to get at the back of the bird's head in the first place? I think the most likely explanation is that the caracal found the ostrich either already dead, or so weak that it was unable to raise its head.

With good reason the caracal is known for its ferocity. One night we were watching three jackals feeding on a springhare kill when a caracal ran in among them, hissing and spitting, and split them apart; it was as if they had been hit by a ball of fire. The jackals retired some distance and after a few minutes regrouped and stormed the caracal. The cat sat on its haunches and spat and cuffed at the jackals, which soon called off the attack and retreated. Poetic justice followed: half an hour later the caracal was in turn chased off the food by a brown hyaena.

I have seen brown hyaenas rob caracals of food more often than I have seen any other carnivores steal from each other. In light of this, it seems strange that caracals rarely take their kills into trees. I have seen or heard of this only once.

African wild cat or small spotted cat?

T HE African wild cat or *vaalbos-kat* looks for all the world like a domestic cat. This is not surprising since it was the African wild cat that the ancient Egyptians began domesticating more than 3 000 years ago; they considered it sacred. Although today, the domestic cat and the African wild cat are separate species, cross-breeding takes place and presents a problem, since few pure populations of African wild cat remain in Africa. Even in the Kalahari Gemsbok National Park the occasional domestic cat turns up and the result is hybrid kittens.

It should come as no surprise that rats and mice are the most common food of the wild cat. They also eat sunspiders, locusts, small reptiles and birds. Hares and springhares are the largest prey known to have been taken by wild cats.

The wild cat is a classical "sit-and-wait" predator. A well known one used to lie in wait in a small hollow at Cubitje Quap windmill and pounce on doves as they alighted at sunset to drink. I once watched another wild cat moving through a patch of *driedoring* bushes in the early morning. The cat had stopped to watch a whistling rat feeding some two metres away when suddenly another rat scurried down a hole. The cat moved over and sat quietly near the mouth of the hole, curling its tail around its body in typical cat fashion. After a wait of about two minutes, the cat pounced and caught the rat as it reappeared from the hole.

Wild cats are skilled tree climbers and will scuttle up a tree when chased. I saw a brown hyaena chase a wild cat for 150 m; the cat raced for a large tree and was up the trunk and onto a branch in a flash. They will also sometimes spend the day sleeping in a tree.

The Kalahari supports a number of African wild cats and they are often seen during the day.

Not so the small spotted cat. Although the literature indicates that the small spotted cat occurs in the Kalahari, I have not yet seen one, despite working in the park and spending many hours driving around at night using a spotlight. The only small spotted cat I have seen was a dead one on the road near Middelburg, Cape. The thing which impressed me most was the large size of its canine teeth.

The small spotted cat, also known as the black-footed cat, is a close relative of the African wild cat and is sometimes confused with the African wild cat, which also has black feet. The new name, small spotted cat, will cause less confusion. While the African wild cat is common throughout its wide range, which takes in all of Africa except the harshest deserts and the tropical forests, the small spotted cat is a good deal less common. Even though it is confined to the arid interior of southern Africa, one's chances of seeing a small spotted cat are slim.

CHAPTER SIX

Other carnivores

BESIDES the hyaenids and felids, three more carnivore families have representatives in the Kalahari. They are the canids — jackals, wild dogs and foxes; the closely related mustelids — badgers and polecats; and the viverrids — suricates, mongooses and genets.

Jackals - the most eclectic eaters

THE arch-opportunist among the Kalahari carnivores must be the black-backed jackal. Jackals can take advantage of many different situations: they can be active by day or night; they can scavenge or they can hunt; they can eat almost any kind of invertebrate or subsist on wild fruits; they can forage on their own or join 30 others eating a carcass.

Jackals stay around lions or hyaenas, feeding at a carcass, and are adept at snatching a morsel whenever opportunity occurs. Occasionally, a lion will seize a jackal that becomes too bold, usually killing it with one bite. More often, jackals wait for the remains after lions have finished feeding. Scavenging from a carcass which is being eaten by hyaenas is not as dangerous — especially towards the end when most of the hyaenas are becoming satiated. Jackals sometimes even have the audacity to nip a hyaena's back legs, which usually results in the hyaena immediately spinning around and the jackal jumping smartly out of the way.

During the height of the springbok rut in June and July, it is not unusual to find some springbok rams with severe injuries, such as a broken leg, as a result of territorial battles. Springbok are also prone to mange, which reduces their mobility. Such springbok may be attacked and killed by small packs of jackals. During the springbok lambing season, pairs of jackals move through the springbok herds looking for lambs; their success at catching lambs depends on a cooperative effort. One jackal distracts the mother while the other goes for the lamb. During dry winter months, especially during periods of drought when the large antelope start dying of starvation, up to 20 jackals may collect around a carcass.

Jackals are accomplished hunters of springhares, rats and mice, and will also feed on birds' eggs, small reptiles, beetles, locusts and other insects. When a termite eruption takes place, termites leave their nest in thousands in an attempt to establish new colonies. A jackal or two brought home to me one night while I was sitting near a springbok carcass, which I hoped would attract brown hyaenas. After dark, the expected pair of jackals appeared. They started nibbling one of the haunches but, not wishing to disturb any brown hyaenas which might be near, I did not chase them away. Besides, I thought, there was plenty of meat. will invariably be there to feed on the easy-to-get and highly nutritious, protein-rich termites as they begin their nuptial flights. Jackals even eat fruit; during the fruiting season their faeces are full of pips from the berries of the brandybush (*Grewia flava*).

The speed at which jackals dispose of a carcass is deceptive. This was

After a few minutes one of the jackals trotted off. It soon returned and the other moved off. For the next hour or so there was a constant coming and going of jackals from the carcass. Eventually I decided to follow to see what they were doing. One jackal moved away several hundred metres and then started digging frantically with its forefeet. After it had dug for a few seconds, I saw it deposit into the hole a piece of meat which it had been carrying in its mouth. It covered the hole by pushing sand in with its snout, then returned to the carcass.

Gradually I realised that there were, in fact, four jackals feeding on the carcass, never more than two at a time, and that although the skin around the haunches was still intact, they had bored out all the meat, as mice do when they gnaw into a large piece of cheese. In short order, these jackals had deprived any foraging brown hyaenas of a substantial amount of food. Meat they could not eat on the spot was hoarded.

Black-backed jackals have a strange mobbing call which is rather a high-pitched bark, "Waa ... waa ... waa ...," repeated over and over again. This is directed at other carnivores, especially leopards.

Early one morning we were listening to the mobbing call of a jackal when suddenly there was silence. A few moments later we saw a leopard walking with a seemingly dead jackal hanging from its mouth. Half an hour later we followed the leopard's spoor. After more than a kilometre, the tracks led to a bush under which the leopard had placed the jackal. Then, to our surprise, the jackal suddenly got up and ran off, somewhat shaken and with its neck a little ruffled.

The basic unit of black-backed jackal society is the monogamous pair, which defends a territory. Males, averaging 7,5 kg, tend to be slightly larger than females (6,8 kg), but it is almost impossible to tell the sex of an animal in the field. Only when a pair of jackals is on a scent-marking spree is this feasible; the male raises its leg to urinate, whereas the female squats.

Jackals are seasonal breeders, producing their young in early summer. They go to earth in small holes where three or four pups are born and remain until they are old enough to move about. At first the pups can be seen at the entrance to the hole waiting for the parents' return to feed them. As they grow bigger the pups venture further afield, but they usually stay together until they are nearly full-grown.

Occasionally some of the previous year's young remain with the parents and help to feed the new pups. It has been shown in East Africa that the number of pups surviving from a litter is directly related to the number of jackal "helpers", another case of kin selection (animals helping their relatives to survive at the cost of reproducing themselves).

The bat-eared fox – an insect fancier

DURING winter, one often sees three or four buffy-grey, dog-like creatures with rounded backs, black bushy tails and enormous ears, moving with their ears pointed forward and down and their noses to the ground. So preoccupied are they that, by staying quiet, it is possible to get really close to them. Every so often one will stop, dig rapidly with its forefeet for a few seconds, and then eat something. Alternatively, one may start moving back and forth, picking up small food items.

These are bat-eared foxes, foraging for two of their favourite foods — beetle larvae, which are dug out, and harvester termites, which the foxes pick up from the ground.

Harvester termites become active only when it is warm enough. They are unique amongst termites in that they have black, pigmented heads which allow them to forage above ground during the day and not be burnt by the sun. Thus, in winter, when it is too cold for them to be active at night, they forage by day; and in the summer, when it is too hot to be about during the day, they turn to a nocturnal existence.

Similarly, bat-eared foxes transpose their activity cycles between summer and winter so as to be active at the same time as their important prey insects.

Although highly favoured, termites and beetle larvae are not the only prey of the bat-eared fox. Beetle adults, locusts, scorpions, small mice and wild berries are other important items of food. These little foxes have large dish-shaped ears which act as parabolic reflectors, amplifying the slightest sound, enabling them to find their prey at night or underground.

Bat-eared foxes, which weigh around 4 kg, are extraordinarily nimble on their feet and are able to double back on their tracks very suddenly and to twist and dodge at high speeds. This is a great help when they are escaping from predators. We once watched a leopard stalking a group of 11 bat-eared foxes. When the leopard got close enough, it charged and quickly singled out a fox.

The leopard was closing in fast on the fox and was about to grab it when the fox did a right-angled turn without any change of pace. By the time the leopard had applied its brakes enough to turn, the fox was well out of harm's way. The foxes then bunched together, uttering high-pitched barks, and followed the leopard closely as it moved off quickly and jumped into a tree.

When pursued by a brown hyaena, bat-eared foxes often behave in an even more distracting manner. Not only does the pursued fox twist and dodge, but other foxes will cut in front of the hyaena in an attempt to distract it and save their fellow creature. It seems that the reason bat-eared foxes go around in small groups is not, like lions and spotted hyaenas, to co-operate in catching food; rather, the foxes co-operate so that *they* are not caught as food.

As a rule bat-eared foxes are monogamous, forming a very strong pair bond which may last for life, although occasionally a male may mate with two females. Like jackals, they give birth to litters of from two to six in early summer, sometimes raising two litters at a den simultaneously. The den is a small hole in the ground, usually a disused aardvark or springhare hole adapted to their requirements, with several entrances. The parents share parental duties.

At sunset, the mother nurses her cubs before setting out for a long foraging search lasting, perhaps, 10 hours. Because of increased energy demands for producing milk, she needs to be able to obtain a good supply of food. At sunrise she returns to the den to give the cubs another drink. The father, on the other hand, spends less time looking for food, but stays near the den guarding the cubs. He also goes with the cubs when they begin looking for food themselves.

During high rainfall years, bat-eared foxes are extremely common. It was usual to see 30 or more on a drive of 40 km along the Nossob riverbed from Nossob camp northwards during the wet cycle of the 1970s. During dry years they disappear and we would be lucky if we saw four foxes along the same drive in the early 1980s. However, in July 1982, the Kalahari received unseasonal winter rains which caused a brief surge of termite activity. For about a week afterwards as many as 12 bat-eared foxes were seen along the above-mentioned drive, only to disappear again. Their disappearance during dry conditions seems to result from two causes — movement into the dunes and high mortality.

The elegant Cape fox

THE smallest canid in the Kalahari is, in my opinion, also the most beautiful. It is the Cape or silver fox (confusingly known in Afrikaans as both *silwervos* and *silwerjakkals*). Weighing no more than 3 kg and possessing a large bushy tail which makes up more than a third of its total length, this dainty little nocturnal animal is the only true fox found in southern Africa.

Cape foxes are remarkably agile, possibly even more so than their bat-eared cousins. The tail serves as a counterbalance for the rest of the body while it twists and turns at high speed to avoid capture. The tail also serves as a decoy, drawing the attention of the pursuer away from the fox's body and its direction of travel.

Although they generally hunt alone, Cape foxes live in pairs or small groups of related individuals, which defend a common territory. They breed in early summer, which is also the best time to see these engaging little animals. In the early morning and late afternoon the adults may be seen lying at their dens and the cubs often come out to play as well.

Insects such as beetles and termites, small rodents and lizards are the Cape fox's main food in the Kalahari. Some foxes occasionally enter Nossob camp to feed on the pods of the exotic mesquite trees growing there and to lick the plates of untidy campers. Once I saw a Cape fox run down and kill a hare; but, in hours spent sitting at carcasses, I never saw a Cape fox show any interest in carrion, so scavenging is apparently not important to them.

Wild dogs are roamers

WILD dogs are the rarest large carnivore in the Kalahari. We were therefore delighted when a pack of eight dogs settled in the south of the park, near Twee Rivieren, in 1974. Then one fateful day in February 1975, they left the park and entered farming areas to the south. Within 24 hours two had been shot, after which the remaining six returned to the park.

Fearing that they might again leave the park with similar disastrous consequences, we decided to try and catch them so that they could be released near Nossob camp in the centre of the park. This operation, however, was not very successful; we lost one wild dog during the capture operation and when we released the remaining five the pack split up. Three were not seen again and two males remained in the area only a few months before they, too, disappeared. I once saw these two dogs feeding on a bat-eared fox they had just killed. To my knowledge this is the first record of wild dogs feeding on another canid.

During the next few years there were a handful of sightings of wild dogs in the Kalahari Gemsbok National Park. My next encounter with wild dogs was with a single young female, which entered Nossob camp early one morning in December 1978. After that I had to wait another two years before experiencing perhaps the most unexpected incident of my twelve years in the Kalahari.

I was following two spotted hyaenas along the Nossob riverbed above Leijersdraai. Conditions were very dry and there was no game in sight. It was four o'clock in the morning, I was feeling sleepy and was beginning to wonder if it was worthwhile punishing myself and my mother-in-law, who was with me, any longer. Suddenly, the hyaenas veered to one side. In the moonlight we saw eight wild dogs running towards them. The dogs did not pursue the hyaenas, however, and the hyaenas stopped about 50 metres away and stood looking back at the wild dogs.

The dogs for their part quickly lost interest in the hyaenas, but were extremely interested in the truck. They came right up to it and, even when I shone a spotlight on them, they showed no concern. This was probably the first time they had ever seen a vehicle.

I decided to remain with the dogs and when the hyaenas moved on we stayed behind. A few minutes later we noticed more movement in the direction from which the dogs had come. I switched on the spotlight and there, moving slowly towards us, were another 15 wild dogs; four adults accompanied by eleven pups, each about one third the size of an adult dog.

Wild dogs are normally regarded as diurnal and it was a surprise to see them active at night. They had full stomachs and blood around their faces and had obviously just come from a kill. There was a full moon at the time, which may have accounted for their nocturnal activities.

After the pups and the rest of the adult dogs had got used to the truck, the pack lay down and went to sleep around the vehicle. At daybreak they began to stir. At first one or two got up, stretched and started grooming themselves. Gradually, the entire pack followed their example and soon all 23 were gambolling around the vehicle, chasing one another back and forth, the white tips of their tails striking in the early light.

A few of the adults started ranging out independently in different directions, stopping to survey the surroundings. At this stage a brown hyaena was seen making its way along the road some 200 metres away. The hyaena did not appear to notice the dogs; and the dogs showed only mild interest in the hyaena. This contrasted to their reaction earlier when they had seen the spotted hyaenas. Spotted hyaenas compete with wild dogs and often steal their food, whereas brown hyaenas pose no threat to wild dogs.

A lone gemsbok approached, took one look at the dogs and quickly departed in the opposite direction.

Eventually the dogs started moving off, closing ranks as they did so. The direction they took was back into the dunes in the Botswana section of the park. After they had been travelling for half an hour, one flushed a steenbok which was immediately pursued by six of the adults. Within a kilometre they had caught it. The steenbok doubled back as the leading dog lunged at it, only to be caught by those coming up behind. Within a few seconds the bleating stopped as the dogs tore the steenbok apart.

We then witnessed one of the most remarkable traits in the behaviour of these fascinating creatures. The pups came running up to the six feeding adults which immediately left the food for the little ones. Wild dogs are the only carnivores that allow their young to eat before the adults.

One steenbok does not go far among so many ravenous mouths, and within five minutes of its being killed all that was left were legs, the skull and some skin.

Soon after this incident a small pack of wild dogs settled around Nossob camp and were seen intermittently in the area, even managing to raise pups. They also caught the one and only impala which had lived in the park for five years. They have not been seen since February 1984.

It is puzzling that there are not more wild dogs in the southern Kalahari. The open habitat and abundant supply of springbok would appear to provide ideal habitat for Africa's rarest large carnivore. But for reasons not yet understood wild dogs are great roamers and their numbers are given to wide fluctuations.

Honey badgers forage two ways

THE honey badger, or *ratel*, is the larger of the two mustelids found in the Kalahari. Although stories abound of the ferocity and truculence of this 10-kg bundle of fury, it is on the whole a shy animal and quickly runs off and into a hole if approached too closely by a vehicle. However, when pressed and unable to bolt down a hole, a badger will soon turn and face an attacker. Uttering a harsh sound — its mouth wide open, exposing its not insignificant teeth — it will make repeated charges.

Honey badgers are often about during daylight. In the Kalahari, particularly during the cooler winter months, one or a pair may be seen trotting along, seemingly oblivious to everything going on around them, unless it is of direct importance to them. From downwind they can be approached very closely.

As their name implies honey badgers are partial to honey and will rip apart beehives, apparently immune to the stings of bees. Bees do occur in the Kalahari, but I have never seen or heard of a honey badger raiding a hive and they eat a variety of other foods.

Honey badgers forage in two different ways. On the one hand they move comparatively small distances, seven or so kilometres in a 24-hour period, meandering considerably and frequently stopping to dig. They are searching for small food items, particularly mice and scorpions, but also small reptiles and beetles. Alternatively they move more directly, covering three times the distance in the same time, but hardly stopping to dig. In this instance, they are on the lookout for larger prey, such as snakes, hares and foxes.

They are frequently accompanied by several chanting goshawks. Two or more goshawks, especially if perched low on bushes, are often a sign that there are honey badgers about. The goshawks collect around the honey badgers as they start digging, ready to snap up any little animal which escapes the badgers. Sometimes a jackal or two will also join the feeding party to see what can be had. The honey badgers take little notice of these fellow foragers.

This is not always the case with other predators, however. Cases have been recorded of a honey badger chasing an aardwolf for some distance until the latter escaped down a hole, and of a honey badger unsuccessfully chasing a group of bat-eared foxes. We also found one which had robbed a wild cat of its spring-hare prey, and, even more audacious, one which had stolen a steenbok from a brown hyaena. The hyaena later recovered the carcass as the badger could not find a large enough hole to take the steenbok down.

It is possible that the two foraging strategies are linked to the sex of the animal — the larger males hunting over longer distances, and the females keeping their eyes closer to the ground on shorter forays. Males appear to have larger territories than females. A male we followed for several days moved over an area of 174 sq km, whereas a female and her daughter lived in an area of 54 sq km.

The females raise their young on their own and, even when the cubs are half-grown, they spend all their time with their mother, although they do catch some food for themselves. They follow her closely and when she digs, they often lie down just behind her, hoping to be fed a mouse or whatever else she might dig out.

Honey badgers are accomplished hole-diggers, equipped with extremely powerful front feet and claws. Much of their prey is dug out of the ground. Even a hard riverbed is no problem for a honey badger. On several occasions I have seen a badger dig a hole so large that it has disappeared completely in a few minutes. Digging is such second nature to them that they often dig a hole in which to sleep for the day; this in spite of the Kalahari having an abundant supply of holes of all shapes and sizes. Honey badgers are also capable tree-climbers and will scale a tree with a vertical trunk without difficulty.

Mustelids are well known for the strong smell they give off from their anal glands. I experienced this when four spotted hyaenas I was following encountered a honey badger. The badger jumped into a tree, but somehow lost its grip and fell out among the hyaenas. The next instant there was a loud rattling sound and a foul smell from the badger, which immediately caused the hyaenas to jump back.

The badger ran off pursued by one of the hyaenas, then stopped, lifted its tail and turned to face the hyaena, again baring its teeth, rattling, and emitting a foul smell. The hyaena jumped back and the honey badger moved on, followed at a less enthusiastic pace by the hyaena. Once again, the badger used its remarkable defence mechanism on the hyaena. This proved too much and the hyaena left the badger to continue on its way. Lions, too, are reputedly repelled by this form of chemical defence.

Striped polecats – celebrated scent ejectors

THE striped polecat is a tiny skunk-like nocturnal carnivore. Males weigh about 900 grams and the females are about a third smaller. They are solitary and feed on a wide range of small animals. The richly black and white striped back is possibly a warning colouration as they are also celebrated scent ejectors.

Although I once saw a brown hyaena kill and eat a striped polecat, they and spotted hyaenas usually maintain a respectful distance from these mustelids. I have seen a spotted hyaena toss a striped polecat as if it were too hot to handle; on landing, the polecat rolled over and ran into a hole. A more significant predator of the striped polecat is the giant eagle owl. I have twice flushed eagle owls eating polecats; on both occasions the polecat was eaten head first.

The sociable suricate

DESPITE some physical resemblance to the mustelids, the viverrids are in fact more closely related to the hyaenas and cats. Evidence for this can be found by comparing skulls and from chromosomal and fossil studies.

The suricate or *meerkat* is the most common of the park's viverrids, particularly along the dry riverbeds. These alert and inquisitive little animals are often seen standing up on their hind legs, leaning back on their tails as if these were shooting sticks, with their front paws held out to the fore as they scan their surroundings. Then they drop down onto all fours and race off with their slender black-tipped tails standing straight up in the air. It is believed that the erect tails serve to keep the group together more easily. Black patches around their eyes make them look as if they are wearing sunglasses.

Suricates weigh between 700 and 900 g. They are highly social animals, living in groups which vary in size from three to 30 individuals.

They sleep in burrows with many entrances, either digging these themselves, or making use of ground squirrel holes. Often they share a warren with a family of ground squirrels for the night; on these occasions, the ground squirrels do not appear to show any antagonism to their visitors. Unless there are very small young, a group of suricates may not occupy the same warren every night but, at the end of the day seek out a suitable refuge.

Early next morning, after a careful look around, they leave for a day's foraging. If the weather is cold they sit around on their haunches sunbathing, their bellies facing the rising sun. Despite their apparently dozy state, at least one mounts constant guard, its head continually turning in all directions to spot possible danger.

Every few hundred metres in their territory suricates have a set of holes. They move from the vicinity of one set of holes to the next, often giving each hole a quick dig-out when they arrive. Nearly all the time one member of the group acts as a guard, foregoing all attempts at finding food. Instead, it climbs to some promontory which may be a tree stump, fallen branch, bush, or antheap. It then has a good view of the surroundings and for half an hour or so it will scan the area for signs of danger. As soon as it has had enough it climbs down and its place is immediately taken by another member of the group.

While there is a guard on duty, the other members of the group give their undivided attention to foraging. When, for some or other reason, there is no guard on duty, their foraging is often disturbed and they are then seen frequently on their back legs, nervously scanning the area. At the first sign of danger, the one who has seen the intruder chatters the alarm and they all rush to the nearest holes.

The major enemies of suricates are the larger birds of prey, particularly martial and tawny eagles. In spite of the suricates' high level of vigilance, I have twice seen a martial swoop down and pick one up and Clem Haagner has seen tawny eagles bring in suricates to their nest. Not only does attack come from the air; terrestrial carnivores, such as black-backed jackals and honey badgers also take suricates.

The long front claws of the suricates are ideally suited for digging and when foraging, they frequently pause to dig. The speed at which they excavate is phenomenal; it is like watching an old-time motion picture. Beetle larvae and scorpions are their favourite foods, and they are among the few animals that will eat the large millipedes that are so common in the Kalahari after rain. The millipedes eject a defensive, repulsive fluid, but somehow the suricates are able to deal with this.

Young are mainly born during the summer months. When they are very small one of the group members, but not the mother of the cubs, stays at home to guard the young while the others go off foraging. At this time the mother is apparently excused all guarding duties so that she can forage as much as possible to enhance her milk production.

I once watched a group of 12 suricates approach some Cape foxes lying at their den at sunset. As the suricates approached, they bunched tightly together and advanced with their tails up, looking like one large animal. The adult fox paid little attention to them, but two cubs were intensely interested. Several times, when the cubs approached too closely, the suricates mass-chased them and the youngsters ran off with tails between their legs. After investigating two of the holes at the warren, all the suricates disappeared for the night down a hole which was not being used by the foxes.

Mongooses rely on cover

T HE two species of mongoose commonly found in the Kalahari are the yellow and the slender mongoose. Neither has anything like the complex social organisation of the suricate. They are much more solitary foragers, although yellow mongooses tend to live in small groups which come together at the warrens.

They are both slightly lighter than suricates, the yellows weighing about 600 g and the slenders about 500 g. The distinguishing features of the yellow mongoose are the white tip to its fairly bushy tail and the tawny yellow colour of the fur on its upper parts. The slender mongoose has a black-tipped tail and the body colour of the Kalahari form is a beautiful bright auburn, as opposed to more brindled colouration found in other areas.

The diet of the yellow mongoose is similar to that of the suricate, except that yellow mongooses are not such avid diggers and feed more on invertebrates living above ground, such as locusts and termites. Yellow mongooses also eat a few larger animals like mice and small reptiles. Slender mongooses are more dependent on mice and reptiles and have been known to attack and kill even large and poisonous snakes.

Why should suricates be such so-cial animals, and yellow and slender mongooses so solitary? The chief advantage to be gained from being social is that it is far safer for an individual to be in a group than on its own. One member of the group is routinely on the lookout for danger, and each member's chances of being caught are lowered by having the others around.

Suricates live in open habitat along riverbeds or on pans where their predators can easily detect them. On the other hand, yellow and slender mongooses live in more concealed areas; yellow mongooses live mainly among tall grasses in the dunes, and slender mongooses spend much of their time foraging around fallen trees or among calcrete outcrops. The habitats of the yellow and slender mongoose, therefore, give them far more protection from predators. This in turn gives them the advantage of foraging alone and of not having to share any rich food patches with others of their kind.

A new discovery – banded mongoose

R ECENTLY a third species of mongoose was recorded along the Nossob riverbed. In 1983 film makers Richard Goss and Tony Bannister saw five banded mongooses near Nossob camp. When they told me about it I exercised my usual scepticism for this sort of report. However, both Richard and Tony are experienced naturalists and their sighting had to be taken seriously.

A few weeks later Richard again reported seeing the banded mongooses, some 15 km from the first location, and that they had gone into a hole for the night. Early the next morning we were at the scene and I was thrilled to see them myself. The nearest record of a banded mongoose is at Okwa, some 350 km to the north.

Small-spotted genet – rarely seen

THE largest of the viverrids found in the Kalahari is the small-spotted genet. This lithe, long-bodied creature weighs about 2 kg and is so strictly nocturnal that it is rarely seen by visitors. Genets spend much of their time in trees, but come down onto the ground to hunt small rodents which are their most important prey. They also eat locusts, scorpions, sun-spiders and small reptiles. They appear to be solitary animals; the only ones I have seen together have been a mother and her young.

This genet is mainly an occupant of dry country, occurring in the Sudan and Sahel, Algeria and Morocco, and parts of Europe and the Middle East as well as in southern Africa.

CHAPTER SEVEN

Birds can fly

THE fact that birds can fly has special significance in the Kalahari. They can easily cover great distances, and many species are thus able to take advantage of favourable conditions seasonally or occasionally, even though they could not survive here all the time.

The result is that of the 264 species recorded in the Kalahari Gemsbok National Park, only 78 are residents (always present). Sixteen species are regular seasonal migrants. Another 18 are classified as nomads, meaning that they visit the Kalahari regularly but not at any predictable season. And the great majority of species recorded (152) are vagrants — irregular visitors which may be common in some years, depending on conditions.

The seed-eating nomads

NOMADIC birds are the most abundant. Larks, finch-larks, canaries, weavers, wattled starlings, sandgrouse and doves come and go in their thousands. These birds are inhabitants of a vast area known as the south-west arid region of southern Africa — including most of Namibia, Namaqualand, the Karoo and the Kalahari — and are mainly seed-eaters. If it rains, seeds are abundant, but if the rains fail, seeds are almost entirely absent. The birds are constantly on the move, seeking out areas where conditions are best, and exploiting them for as long as possible, which may be from a few days to several months. Then the birds move on.

Although seeds are good food, they are usually without moisture. Seed-eating birds, in order to survive, must drink. Doves and sandgrouse collect in large numbers at waterholes, the doves at sunrise and sunset, the sandgrouse about two hours after sunrise. It is worth noting that the provision of artificial water has meant that doves and sandgrouse are able to spend much longer periods in the Kalahari than before these waterholes were made.

The gathering of large numbers of birds at certain waterholes attracts several predators. Lanner and red-necked falcons often hunt around waterholes, as do black-backed jackals and African wild cats, so that birds coming to drink face danger from air and on the ground.

Doves and sandgrouse carry water to their chicks. The doves carry water in their crops and regurgitate it on arrival at the nests, but the sandgrouse has evolved a different method. Sandgrouse males are equipped with special chest feathers which can absorb water. During the nesting period, the male enters the water and soaks these feathers. In this way, the male sandgrouse is known to carry water as far as 80 km. When he comes to the nest the chicks gather round and "spoon" the water from the wet feathers in their tiny bills.

Other seed-eaters supplement their diet with insects, especially when feeding their young. Insects, too, are a source of moisture. Many birds can do without water by eating both seeds and insects. A few select species, such as the scalyfeathered finch, survive exclusively on seeds, without having to add insects to their diet.

Residents must breed

IN THE Kalahari the resident bird species are chiefly raptors, like the chanting and gabar goshawks, martial and tawny eagles, or insectivores, such as the Marico and chat flycatchers. the striking crimson-breasted shrike, the forktailed drongo and the familiar and anteating chats. A few mixed feeders (insects and fruits) such as the redeyed bulbul, pied barbet, and Cape and Burchell's glossy starlings are also common residents. The resident species do not reach the numbers of the nomads because they live off a lower density, although more predictable, food supply than seeds.

Because the food supply is nevertheless erratic, most birds resident in the Kalahari do not have a fixed breeding season; they breed opportunistically after rain. A shower of 20 mm is all that is necessary to trigger breeding. For some species the lag between the first good rainfall and the first eggs being laid can be as little as seven days. The birds continue breeding until the food supply falls to the danger point where egg production and feeding of the young are no longer possible.

The duration of a breeding period depends not only on the amount of rain, but on the time of year rain falls. If rain comes early and is not followed by other wet periods to maintain growth, the vegetation dries out; in this event insects disappear and bird breeding stops. Nestlings die in the nests as parents and helpers cannot sustain them. Late summer rains, on the other hand, have a more lasting effect on the vegetation and this enables the birds to continue breeding into the winter.

Courser withstands overheating

A BIRD superbly adapted to the erratic Kalahari environment is the plover-like doublebanded courser. It does not need any drinking water and can withstand extreme overheating without noticeable distress. It is even reported to move away from areas where rain has fallen, since shrubs and tall grasses cut down visibility; the courser seems to like barren conditions best of all.

The doublebanded courser is one of the few birds that breeds throughout the year, irrespective of conditions; each time it lays only one egg. During a year a single bird will lay three or four eggs and, in this way, overcome the low reproduction rate from a small clutch.

The manner in which a constant temperature around the egg is maintained is another remarkable feature of this bird's behaviour. At temperatures below 30°C, both parents alternate at incubating the egg to keep it warm. Between 30°C and 36°C, however, they merely shade it. Above 36°C, they incubate it again, now to withdraw heat from the egg.

As they nest in open places on the ground, doublebanded coursers are directly exposed to the sun. During incubation in midsummer, they suffer high temperatures which they are not able to regulate; they simply allow their body temperature to rise. However, every hour or so, they have nest relief when the other parent takes over. In this way, each parent has a turn of duty in the sun, followed by a period of rest in the shade where it sheds excess heat before returning to the egg.

Korhaan and bustard displays

THE most conspicuous bird in the Kalahari dunes is the black korhaan. The strikingly coloured black and white males make a raucous cackling as they execute their apparently unending display flights by day and night; this is one of the most dramatic courtships in the Kalahari.

Less often seen, but even more spectacular, is the display flight of the redcrested korhaan. The bird starts off on the ground by clacking its bill. Then a penetrating whistle accompanies the clacking. As the sounds reach a crescendo the bird flies almost vertically upwards, perhaps 30 m, then suddenly tumbles over and drops to the ground, as if shot. When the bird seems about to strike the ground, it suddenly spreads its wings and glides some distance away to settle.

Related to the korhaans is the kori bustard which, at 15 kg, is the heaviest flying bird in the world. Kori bustards feed on seeds, insects, small reptiles and mammals; they also like locusts, crickets and termites. They are fond of the gum of acacia trees; hence their Afrikaans name *gompou*. During the breeding season the males strut about impressively with necks puffed out, wings pointed downwards and tails fanned out. Before dawn their great call, which sounds like the distant sonic boom of an aircraft, can be heard.

Life at communal nests

A FEATURE peculiar to the Kalahari landscape, especially along the riverbeds, is the large thatched-roof shapes in many camelthorn trees. These are the nest masses of sociable weavers which live in huge colonies of up to 300 birds. Each colony builds and occupies one or more nest masses. The nest mass, which is divided into chambers, is a structure which lasts as long as the branch upon which it is built can sustain its weight. Eventually — weighed down by the ever-increasing nest mass and also affected by strong winds — the branch cracks and the whole structure comes crashing down.

During breeding, each pair of birds has its own nesting chamber where the chicks remain until they can fly, when they are about three weeks old. When sociable weavers are not breeding, the nests are still used by the birds, as they provide protection from the midday summer sun and the night-time winter cold. At such times, occupation of the nest chambers is on a first come, first served, basis.

Unlike most birds, which start incubating their eggs only after all have been laid, sociable weavers start incubating their eggs immediately the first one is laid. This results in eggs hatching out at different times. If food becomes scarce, the brood size is quickly reduced by the deaths of the youngest chicks, which cannot compete for the food with older siblings. The young of first broods help their parents to feed the young of second and subsequent broods.

While communal nests provide refuge from the weather, the weavers are still at risk from some predators. Cape cobras are able to raid the nest chambers without difficulty and are reported to take a heavy toll of eggs and young during the breeding season. Honey badgers may also climb some of the nesting trees and destroy the nest masses with their strong front legs to gobble up any chicks that are around.

Often the entrances to some of the nest chambers are rimmed by white droppings. This is evidence that the nest is also occupied by a pair of pygmy falcons. The smallest raptor in Africa, no more than 20 cm long, this falcon is often mistaken for a shrike.

If sociable weavers are occupying a nest mass and a pair of falcons moves in, the weavers will not desert unless, as sometimes happens, the falcons take over most of the chambers. The weavers will even breed in chambers adjacent to the falcons. But the weavers do resent the intrusion. Whenever a pygmy falcon appears, the weavers immediately voice their alarm calls until the falcon is out of sight inside a nest chamber, or is far away from the nest.

Sand lizards are the chief food of the pygmy falcon. These they seize from a conspicuous perch. Occasionally, pygmy falcons prey on sociable weavers, especially the chicks. The weavers, though, may derive benefit from the presence of the pygmy falcons as predation on the falcons has been found to be minimal. Possibly the presence of falcons keeps snakes away and so it is worth the weavers' while to lose the odd member of their colony in return for protection from more fearsome predators like snakes.

A communal nest-builder and cooperative feeder similar to the sociable weaver is the whitebrowed sparrowweaver. These weavers build several untidy nests which look like bundles of straw blown into a camelthorn tree, with stalks projecting in all directions. The colonies are small, usually of half a dozen birds which sleep in different nests, and groups spend the day foraging in small territories around the nest tree. Ownership of the territories is continually proclaimed by loud, unmusical song, usually uttered from a prominent point.

Rain is the stimulus for nest-building with the whitebrowed sparrowweaver. Whenever it rains members of a colony start building, but they do not complete the nest if rain is light and an isolated occurrence. Even if these weavers complete the nest they will not necessarily lay eggs or rear chicks in it.

In each colony, only one female

breeds and she, alone, incubates the eggs. All birds in the colony feed the one or two young, but the most dominant bird gives little help, saving its energy for defending the territory. How much energy is involved in this defence is clear among the white-browed sparrowweavers which inhabit Nossob camp. Daily, they do the rounds of all the windows, hubcaps and mirrors of cars parked at the camp, pecking and calling at each vehicle.

When a hawk or other predator is near a nest which has chicks in it, foraging and feeding stop as the adults mob the predator in an attempt to drive it away. Afterwards the adults make up for lost time by feeding the chicks in rapid succession. It has been estimated that up to 18 per cent of foraging time is lost through interference by raiding predators. Thus, co-operation in feeding the chicks is a real advantage, particularly when food is thinly distributed and predators common.

An unusual case of a bird and a mammal nesting together occurs between the anteating chat and the hyaena. Anteating chats often nest in the roofs of burrows inhabited by hyaenas — brown or spotted — and are tolerated by the hyaenas. The chats benefit from this association because the hyaenas discourage potential predators. The birds may also earn their keep by helping to clear the den of ectoparasites such as fleas, as they often forage around the den.

Ostriches can dehydrate

A KALAHARI bird with special adaptations to life in the heat and dust is the ostrich. Ostriches rarely go into the shade and rarely drink. These huge birds, the males weighing as much as 150 kg, cannot, however, survive on dry food alone. In the absence of surface water they rely on moisture in the vegetation and wild fruits such as tsamas and gemsbok cucumbers. Sometimes they will also eat small vertebrates and invertebrates.

But it is their remarkable physiology which enables them to exist in arid regions. They are able to lose up to 25 per cent of their body weight when dehydrated without suffering any ill effects. Experiments have shown that they are able to keep their body temperature normal when the surrounding air temperature is a sizzling 51°C for as long as 7½ hours. If there is a breeze blowing, they can cool themselves without resorting to water-expensive panting. Instead, by fluffing out their feathers, spreading their wings and exposing their naked legs, so that the breeze reaches the skin, they can use convection and radiation to cool down. Only in the absence of wind and at temperatures above 34°C will they start panting in order to keep cool.

Ostriches are also flexible breeders. They have a breeding peak immediately before the rainy season, and this usually ensures that their chicks have succulent food when they hatch; but they can also respond to unseasonal rainfall, and may thus breed at any time of the year.

One extraordinary thing about these birds is that the females are able to recognise their own eggs. Several females lay up to 13 eggs each in a collective nest which is simply a shallow scrape in the ground. However, only one hen, the major hen, incubates the eggs and she is helped by the male. A complete nest can contain 30 or more eggs, but an ostrich can incubate only about 20 eggs. The surplus eggs are pushed aside, where they are not incubated and decay. The major hen is able to recognise her own eggs and keeps them in the nest, only pushing out eggs of minor hens. Exactly how she knows which are which is unknown. She may notice features of the eggs such as shape, surface texture and size differences, since each bird lays similar eggs of more or less the same size, but different birds lay different sized eggs.

The cock bird, with its dark plumage, typically incubates at night, while the drab female usually occupies the nest during the day. The change over takes place an hour or two before sunset and after sunrise and is accompanied by an elaborate display in which the wings are waved in a circular motion. If danger threatens, the incubating bird stretches its neck flat along the ground (but not into the sand). During the breeding season the males utter a loud, three-phase booming call, the last phase resembling the roar of a lion.

When the chicks hatch, their backs are covered with bristly-looking brindled hedgehog-like feathers. The chicks are exceedingly slow moving and vulnerable to predators, although they are usually well guarded by the adults. At the approach of a potential predator, one of the adults, usually a male, performs a distraction display by feigning a broken wing, endeavouring to lead the predator away from the chicks, which, meanwhile, are being escorted off by the other adult.

One often sees chicks of different ages with one pair of adults. Adults with a brood may abduct chicks from another pair. Why should ostriches take on the responsibility of looking after someone else's offspring? The most likely explanation is that raising chicks requires little effort by the parents since the chicks are able to feed themselves. However, the larger the brood — particularly if it has unrelated offspring in it — the smaller the chances that the parents' own offspring will be killed should a predator attack.

Adult ostriches are seldom caught by predators; cheetahs are probably their main enemies. The birds make up for not being able to fly by being able to run at up to 60 km an hour. They can maintain this speed for long distances, traversing dunes as if they did not exist. In addition they possess a brilliant sidestep that must be the envy of every rugby centre in the country.

Fine raptor viewing

THE Kalahari is an ideal place for observing raptors. Of the 80 species of eagles, hawks, buzzards, kites, falcons, harriers, kestrels, owls and vultures recorded in South Africa, 52, or two-thirds, have been seen in the Kalahari.

The longlegged marching eagle, the secretarybird, is a common Kalahari raptor. Secretarybirds are often seen striding across the veld, usually in pairs, looking for mice and lizards which make up the bulk of their diet. Although snakes, including large and dangerous specimens such as puff adders and cobras, are killed and eaten by secretarybirds, they are not the major food items. Prey is killed by lightning-quick stabs with their long, powerful legs, often with the wings partly opened to keep balance.

During the hot dry season, secretarybirds congregate at certain windmills, particularly Leeudril, Rooiputs and Kijkij in the lower Nossob, where there is sweet water. Concentrations of up to 50 secretarybirds have been recorded.

The nest of the secretarybird is a large flat structure built of sticks and lined with grass, and usually sited on top of a fairly small, isolated tree. Two to three eggs are laid and the chicks spend about three months in the exposed nest. They succeed in standing upright only when they are nearly ready to leave the nest. For most of the time they squat on their knees with their feet in front of them.

Both parents feed the chicks and give them water. This is done by slowly regurgitating the water and allowing it to flow into the chick's upstretched beak. Food is regurgitated into the nest. It seems that the adult is unable to control the amount of food it regurgitates. Once it starts it is unable to stop until it has emptied its stomach. It then will join the chicks in gobbling up the regurgitated food in order to have some sustenance itself.

Chanting goshawks, the smaller gabar goshawk, and the greater kestrel are the most abundant and widespread of the smaller raptors. Chanting goshawks and greater kestrels are easily noticed as they generally perch in prominent places. The gabar goshawk, on the other hand, sits inside the canopy of a tree and flies swiftly from one tree to the next.

The chanting goshawk, with its long orange legs and bill, its finely

barred ashy-grey plumage and, in flight, its striking white primaries, is a handsome bird. However, compared to many raptors, it is almost ungainly and is more of a sit-and-wait predator and hoverer than a swooper. Chanting goshawks feed off a wide variety of reptiles, including large snakes, and also small rodents and insects. I have seen a chanting goshawk attack prey as large as a hare, although I do not know if it made a kill. These raptors follow honey badgers and pirate food from them. They have also been known to take sandgrouse at water.

The dashing gabar goshawk, which at rest looks like a small chanter, feeds mainly on small birds and is well known as a robber of nests. A jet-black melanistic phase of this bird also occurs, but these birds associate freely with birds of the normal colour phase, usually pairing up with one. The greater kestrel, also a hoverer, is mainly an insect eater, grasshoppers being its favourite diet. It is rare among birds in that it sometimes caches its prey. Hiding places in tufts of grass or under stones are usually used as cache sites.

Lanner falcons are frequently found near windmills where they prey on the sandgrouse, doves, and other small birds that come to drink. They fly in fast and low and scatter the birds but they do not have a high success rate. Sometimes a dozen attacks are needed before a quarry is hit. The lanner then picks its victim up and carries it off a little distance, usually eating its meal on the ground.

The smaller rednecked falcon is less common and more difficult to see than the lanner, as it usually sits inside trees; first and last light seem to be the best times for seeing these extremely swift and efficient little predators of other birds.

Eagles, resident and migrant

TAWNY and martial eagles, bateleurs and blackbreasted snake eagles are the common Kalahari eagles. Probably the most inspiring of all is the regal martial eagle. Standing nearly a metre high, with a dark brown head and breast and lightly spotted underparts, this magnificent raptor preys on small mammals, particularly suricates and mongooses, as well as large birds. It soars to a great height, often beyond the range of a man's eyes, and attacks in a long shallow swoop. It is reputed to be able to spot its prey from as far as six kilometres.

In the Kalahari martial eagles often attack kori bustards. Judging by the blood and feathers I once found scattered around a dead kori bustard, victim of a martial eagle, these attacks can lead to a fierce struggle. As with all hunters, learning and experience are of great importance. Clem Haagner watched a juvenile martial eagle make several unsuccessful attempts to catch some small ostriches that had become separated from their parents, and was amazed at the eagle's inefficiency.

The common large brown eagle in the Kalahari is the tawny. Young birds are considerably lighter — almost creamy white — than adults, whose feathers darken to chocolate brown as they grow old. It is a most successful species, feeding on small mammals, reptiles, birds and insects, as well as quite often taking carrion. Like other big eagles, they need stout trees in which to build their large stick nests and so are usually found breeding along riverbeds in the Kalahari. They lay two eggs a few days apart, which results in one chick hatching out earlier. During the first two weeks of their lives the chicks behave aggressively towards each other; the larger one will continually peck at its younger sibling, with the result that the younger chick eventually dies from its injuries. The significance of this Cain and Abel struggle has not been satisfactorily explained.

The most colourful eagle is the bateleur. With its black, grey and brick-red plumage, scarlet lips and face, and stumpy tail, it is unmistakable. In flight, the bateleur rocks slowly from side to side like a tightrope walker and during display flights exhibits a masterly control of the air as it somersaults and rolls; the name bateleur is French for tumbler, juggler, acrobat or tightrope walker. Small mammals, a wide array of birds, and carrion, particularly small carcasses, seem to be their main food. A bateleur was the only visitor in two days to the carcass of a lion-killed spotted hyaena cub.

The blackbreasted snake eagle is easily confused with the martial eagle. The snake eagle is, however, smaller, lacks the dark spots on its belly and is feathered only down to the knees, not to the feet as are the other eagles. As its name indicates, snakes are this bird's most important food and it usually hunts by soaring or hovering, diving on to its prey with claws extended. Small snakes are eaten by the snake eagle as it flies, sometimes being swallowed and then partially drawn out several times before finally disappearing.

Towards the end of the rainy season, during years of high rainfall in the Kalahari, numerous migrant raptors invade the desert. The local population of bateleurs and tawny eagles is joined by others from further afield. In addition, hundreds of steppe eagles, lanner falcons, black kites and yellowbilled kites, redfooted kestrels and whitebellied storks appear, as do lesser numbers of hobbies, peregrines and lesser kestrels. An example of how far these birds may fly was provided by a lanner falcon that was ringed in the Nossob to be recovered six weeks later in Malawi, 2 000 km away.

The steppe eagles come from the Russian steppes and it is thought that some of the tawny eagles and whitebellied storks come from North Africa. All these birds are attracted by masses of winged termites which erupt out of the ground as they embark on their nuptial flight.

As the termites emerge from their holes and flutter into the air they are quickly noticed by a keen-eyed raptor which immediately begins catching as many as it can, swooping in among them and plucking them out of the air with its claws. Other nearby raptors in turn see this behaviour, and soon predatory birds of all different shapes and sizes converge on the mass of protein-rich flying morsels.

The smaller birds, such as falcons, kites and kestrels, catch their prey in the air, whereas the eagles and storks feed on the ground, picking up termites which have shed their wings. At a spectacular termite eruption, there may be as many as 50 to 60 bateleurs, steppe and tawny eagles feeding on the ground, or sitting in trees with bulging crops, while above them in the air swarm scores of smaller raptors.

Vultures and owls

THE common vultures of the Kalahari Gemsbok National Park are the whitebacked vulture and the lappetfaced vulture. In addition, a few whiteheaded vultures probably breed in the area, and the odd immature Cape vulture and hooded vulture are seen. There are also two records of immature palmnut vultures, which may have strayed from breeding grounds in Angola.

Contrary to popular belief vultures cannot survive, at least not in any numbers, on the remains of carnivore kills. Vultures are mainly dependent on carcasses of animals which have met non-violent deaths. Thus, the Kalahari is a good habitat for vultures, except for the Cape vulture which nests on cliffs.

Vultures are efficient foragers. By riding on thermals — the rising currents of warm air generated on the desert floor during the heat of the day — they are able to forage far more widely than mammalian scavengers. Vultures usually locate a carcass before their terrestrial counterparts, and by weight of numbers are able to consume a large carcass within hours. They have excellent vision, enabling them to locate distant carcasses as well as to react when other vultures drop out of the sky onto a meal.

One way scavenging mammals steal a march on vultures is by being nocturnal. This way they find the carcasses of animals which have died at night and can exploit them before the vultures move in. This, along with the fact that it is a good water conservation strategy, is probably the reason the dominant mammalian scavengers, hyaenas, are nocturnal.

Although competitors with hyaenas, vultures are dependent on these animals in an important way: hyaenas provide the much-needed calcium, found in bones, for vultures to feed to their chicks. Because they only eat meat and are unable to break up bones, vultures cannot obtain calcium directly. Therefore they return to carcasses after hyaenas have been feeding. There, they pick up bone splinters left by hyaenas, and carry these back to their chicks. Without this calcium, the chicks' bones would be malformed and they would not be able to fly. Precisely this is occurring in areas where hyaenas have been wiped out by man.

Seven species of owls have been recorded from the Kalahari. The grass owl is a rare visitor in years of exceptionally high rainfall, but the others are all residents. The most common and widespread is the whitefaced owl, which is frequently seen sleeping in thick, branched trees in the rest camps. These owls are fond of arthropods, such as moths and sunspiders. The tiny pearlspotted owl is relatively diurnal and takes many small finch-sized birds.

At the other end of the scale is the giant eagle owl, which takes comparatively large prey such as korhaans, springhares and small carnivores, including the striped polecat. Giant eagle owls can regularly be seen roosting in large camelthorn trees near Twee Rivieren. Their nests are often made on top of a sociable weavers' nest mass. The other three owl species are the barn owl, often heard screeching at night at Nossob camp; the spotted eagle owl — a small rodent specialist, like the barn owl; and the scops owl, which is similar to the whitefaced owl.

Migrants and vagrants

AS INDICATED, several of the 16 migrant species in the Kalahari are raptors, and the remainder are insectivores and shore birds. But by far the majority of bird species recorded from the Kalahari Gemsbok National Park are classed as vagrants — irregular visitors common in some years. Most of these are water birds which visit the seasonal pans in years of good rains. Others are birds that have obviously been blown off course; such unlikely birds as the white pelican, an unidentified phalarope, longtailed skua, buffspotted flufftail, African crake, lesser moorhen, painted snipe, saddlebilled stork, woollynecked stork, palmnut vulture, glossy ibis, African jacana, European sedge warbler, and paradise flycatcher.

CHAPTER EIGHT

The smaller fry

AMONG the smaller creatures of the Kalahari there are interesting adaptations to hot, dry conditions, and facinating interactions between species. Although they may be common and widespread, some of these animals are rarely seen because, besides their small size, many are nocturnal. But they are a vital food source for all the carnivores, from suricates to lions, as well as for predatory birds.

Two unusual and rather strange mammals are the aardvark and pangolin. The aardvark is the only living member of its order Tubulidentata, and is one of the least known of all living mammals. Judging by their spoor and number of holes, they are not uncommon in the Kalahari, but are rarely seen. Pangolins are unique amongst mammals in that, instead of hair, their bodies are covered by horny scales. I have only seen one pangolin in my life, while following a spotted hyaena. Judging by the curiosity ahown by the hyaena I should think that it was the first one she had seen as well. Both aardvarks and pangolins are predominantly ant-eaters.

Two hares (Lagomorphs) occur in the area, although only an expert can tell the difference between the Cape hare and the scrub hare. Predominantly nocturnal, hares are usually only seen on roads at night.

They can run incredibly fast for such small animals and easily reach a speed of 60 km per hour. They obviously need this speed to escape their many predators.

Sixteen species of rodents live in the Kalahari; closely-related species co-existing through having different diets, choices of habitat and periods of the day when they are active, which helps to separate them. Differences in size may result from differences in diet — and Kalahari rodents vary in size from the minute 6-g pygmy mouse to the 12-kg porcupine, 2 000 times larger.

Porcupines – the great burrow diggers

THE porcupine is a common nocturnal Kalahari inhabitant. Roots and bulbs, which they dig out and gnaw, are typical porcupine fare. In order to trim their ever-growing incisors, porcupines gnaw bones. They are avid bone collectors and often carry bones back to their holes. Alternatively, they move into the vacated breeding dens of brown hyaena which, because of the latter's habit of carrying food back for their young, often contain quite an accumulation of bones.

Porcupines are excellent diggers. Over the years some of their hole entrances become enormous, extending downwards through the sand for several metres before the tunnel is reached. The largest holes found in the Kalahari are porcupine palaces which must be many years old. Spotted hyaenas often use porcupine holes for their breeding dens, both sometimes living peacefully together in the same burrow.

Springhares – the survivors

NEXT in size is the considerably smaller springhare (a rodent not a lagomorph), which weighs 3 kg. It resembles the kangaroo and uses a similar means of locomotion; however, it is not even vaguely related to the kangaroo. The resemblance between these animals is an example of convergent evolution: unrelated animals which live in similar environments and have similar habits evolve similar characteristics. A strictly nocturnal animal, the springhare lives on flat open terrain and feeds mainly off the leaves and stems of short grasses.

The springhare is both terrestrial and fossorial (burrowing); it forages above ground and shelters underground. It has a combination of physical features enabling it to live in both habitats. Its terrestrial features include elongated and powerful hind feet, which allow it to move quickly in enormous leaps when chased by a predator, a lengthy tufted tail for counterbalance when jumping, and large ears and eyes for locating predators. (These characteristics are us-ually undeveloped in mainly burrowing mammals, such as the blind, small-eared, stumpy-legged mole-rat.) Modifications for their underground life include slightly valvular nostrils, ears which fold lengthwise along the mid-line to keep out soil, and short, strong, long-clawed front feet for digging.

Springhares live in extensive, multi-entranced burrows made up of a number of inter-connected tunnels which, added together, may extend 140 metres or more. These animals often form feeding groups of several individuals but, when disturbed, each dashes off to its separate burrow system. Only one springhare or, at most, a mother with her single young, has ever been found associated with a particular burrow.

Predator avoidance is an important function of the burrow. The extensive nature of the burrow makes it virtually impossible for a predator to dig out a springhare, and the large number of entrances to the burrow make it easier to get there quickly when emergencies arise.

The burrow is also important in providing shelter from the heat. It provides a micro-environment of moderate temperature and high humidity. It is therefore unnecessary for springhares (and other small burrowing animals) to engage in active heat regulation and use up precious water while in the burrow. To help with cooling, the burrows are usually sited in sandy, relatively porous soils and entrances are often shaded by the only large tree or clump of bushes in an otherwise open area. Also, the many entrances, pointing in different directions and to different wind currents, greatly increase air flow through the burrow.

The springhare's habit of limiting above-ground activity until after dark, when temperatures are lowest and humidity is highest, is important for the conservation of energy and body water. Springhares do not drink water. Their moisture requirements are provided by rain and dew, moisture in their food, and from metabolic water — that is, they make their own water through oxidation of hydrogen in food.

Springhares are born throughout the year and weigh only about 250 g. They remain in their burrows for about seven weeks, totally dependent on their mother's milk, until they reach about one-third adult size. Baby springhares, which are highly vulnerable to predators, never leave the burrow.

Food is not a problem for springhares, even in dry times. They are generally in good physical condition, and high pregnancy and lactation rates occur throughout the year. Unlike most Kalahari animals, whose chief difficulties are getting enough food and water, their biggest problem appears to be avoiding predators. Springhares feed in open areas of short grass, often at distances of 150 m or more from their burrows. They are therefore extremely easy to locate and highly vulnerable to predators. Twenty-one predators of springhares have been documented, ranging from owls to lions.

Ground squirrels – active by day

THE third largest Kalahari rodent — and one visitors are very likely to see — is the 600-g ground squirrel.

Like springhares, the bushy-tailed ground squirrels live in extensive, multi-holed burrows, but they are strictly diurnal and social, usually living in groups of six to twelve animals. They feed mainly on seeds, stems and bases of grass stems, as well as their leaves, and also on tubers and wild fruits.

Ground squirrels spend most of the day foraging above ground, although during very hot periods they may periodically return to their burrows to cool down. They also have several other devices to help regulate temperature. They lie flat on their bellies with their forelegs stretched forwards and the hind legs backwards. This behaviour, appropriately termed hearth rugging, brings the lower body surface in contact with the ground, helping either to warm up or to cool down the squirrel, depending on the season.

They also make ingenious use of their long bushy tails as sunshades, bending their tails over their backs during the heat of the day to provide shade for the head and body; they even turn their bodies to get maximum shade from the tail.

Finally, they have a tough physiological system which ensures that they do not need to drink water. In fact, they possess the most efficient water absorbing kidneys of any mammal that has been studied; this means their urine is highly concentrated, with a minimum of water being lost.

In winter ground squirrels leave their burrows well after sunrise and retire to them about sunset. They therefore escape the severe cold of winter nights by remaining in the burrow, which has an even temperature. Consequently, they rarely have to face temperatures lower than about 10°C, either inside or outside the burrow. On cool and overcast days, the squirrels leave their burrows later and return to them earlier than usual. Ground squirrels thus appear to be far better adapted, behaviourally and physiologically, for going out in the heat than for withstanding the cold.

Birds of prey are their major predators for, like suricates, they are diurnal and live in open habitat which makes them particularly vulnerable to predators. Again like suricates, they try to combat this by being social, which provides more pairs of watchful eyes. They do not, however, have the elegant system of professional guards, as do the suricates. When emerging from their burrows ground squirrels are extremely cautious. They pause with noses just protruding from the burrow until satisfied it is safe to emerge. They have an alarm call, a whistle, which causes a fellow squirrel to dart for the burrow. When pursued they are remarkably agile, throwing their bodies from side to side and using their tails as a foil, in a similar ploy to that used by the Cape fox.

Other rodents

WHISTLING rats are also colonial and diurnal, but are considerably smaller than ground squirrels, weighing about 120 g. Their name is derived from their habit of sitting up on their back legs and emitting a sharp, piercing whistle when sensing danger. They are properly called Brants' whistling rats. Grass seeds and shoots and dwarf shrubs,

particularly *driedoring*, make up the bulk of their diet. The openings to their burrows are invariably covered by a bush and their distribution is closely related to that of the *driedoring*, which is found mainly on compacted sand.

They often carry food back to the burrow and eat it while sitting on the mound or in the opening — an obvious instance of anti-predator behaviour, and probably also useful for thermo-regulatory purposes. They do not have big bushy tails to act as umbrellas and are apparently not as well adapted physiologically to withstand high temperatures as are the ground squirrels. They are not, therefore, able to forage during the heat of the day in summer. As with many rodents, the young cling to their mother's nipples and, therefore, go wherever she goes.

The only other diurnal rodent in the southern Kalahari is the striped mouse which, at a mass of 32 g, is considerably smaller than the whistling rat. As the name implies, these pretty little grey mice have several broad white stripes, flanked with dark hair, running down the length of the back. They feed on grass seeds and annuals, as well as acacia pods. They are solitary animals. Not having any fellows to watch for predators, they are heavily dependent on cover. They seek shelter among thick bushes and shrubs and move very quickly from cover to cover.

The gerbils, small, tawny-coloured rodents with white bellies, are true desert inhabitants and are, perhaps, the most common rodents in the Kalahari. They hop along on their back legs, like springhares. The three most common gerbil species in the Kalahari are the hairy-footed or pygmy gerbil, Highveld or Brants' gerbil, and the Namaqua or short-tailed gerbil. They are all strictly nocturnal, forage in open areas and are seed-eaters. There are considerable differences in size among the three: the largest is Brants' which at 60 g, weighs twice as much as the 30 g of the smallest, the pygmy, and the Namaqua gerbil is about half-way between the two. Accordingly, they do not compete for food, since they feed on seeds of different sizes. They also seem to prefer different substrates. The two smaller ones prefer fine sands, particularly the pygmy gerbil, which is the only rodent able to live on the dune crests where the sand is finest of all. Brants' gerbil, on the other hand, lives mainly on consolidated sand in dune troughs. All gerbils have acute hearing for locating predators — vital for tiny animals which are nocturnal and live in such open areas.

The tree mouse fills a specialised niche in the Kalahari. It is mainly restricted to large trees, especially camelthorns, which can be regarded as habitat islands. It is nocturnal and feeds mainly on acacia seeds and leaves. The tree mouse often builds a large nest, usually above 3 m from the ground, either in the fork of a tree, or as a spherical mass of sticks around branches. It also nests in hollow, fallen tree stumps, or among the stems of blackthorn bushes. The young cling to the female's nipples as she scrambles along the branches.

The strangest looking rodent in the Kalahari is the common molerat. It looks more like a newborn dachshund puppy than a rodent. Tiny eyes, no ears, short legs and tail and a white patch on the top of the head of an otherwise dark, sausage-shaped body, are one's first impression of the molerat. As you get near and it senses you, it lifts its head and exposes two pairs of large incisors. Although they look intimidating, these teeth, together with the big claws on all feet, are mainly used for digging.

Molerats are fossorial; that is, they live most of their lives underground — hence their sausage shape, lack of eyes and ears and strong claws. They are social, living in groups of 20 to 25 which are dominated by a single large breeding female and a dominant male. Each group lives in an extensive burrow system from which the members obtain their food. Most of this comprises roots, bulbs and tubers. Their molehills are large, the soil being pushed out from the tunnel in a mass equal in diameter to the size of the tunnel, and looking like a giant's toothpaste, squeezed from a tube.

During rainy periods, molerats are occasionally seen scurrying about above ground. This may be the time that individuals disperse from their colonies and attempt to start new ones.

Elephant-shrews are not rodents

IF YOU are sitting quietly you may happen to see a small animal sitting under a clump of blackthorn bushes or darting along a runway between bushes. If a closer look at what may at first be mistaken for a rodent reveals that this little animal has a strange nose — very long, thin and pointed and with a highly mobile tip — you have found a bushveld elephant-shrew.

Elephant-shrews are diurnal, insectivorous animals which feed on small invertebrates, such as termites, ants, beetles and grasshoppers. The reason for the strange nose is not really known; one assumes it is important for detecting food, perhaps in sniffing out small creatures among cracks and crevices. It has given rise to the quaint Afrikaans name *klaasneus* for this group of animals. An interesting aspect of this little known animal's behaviour is its habit of drumming a back leg against the ground as an alarm signal to other shrews.

Amphibians and reptiles

IT IS hard to believe that amphibians can survive in a region as arid as the Kalahari. But after heavy rains the world rings out with the chorus of hundreds of small sand frogs (*Tomopterna cryptotis*) and rain frogs (*Breviceps adspersus*). Like the annual plants, these amphibians are quick to get down to the vital task of reproduction when conditions permit.

Even more amazing is the emergence of hundreds of large bullfrogs (*Pyxicephalus adspersus*) during heavy rains. The males of this species are up to 20 cm long, head to tail. They concentrate at large rain pools along riverbeds or on pans, where they set up small territories and compete violently for the smaller females. In the short time available, they must also try to eat as much as they can, which includes practically everything that moves — small birds, rats, reptiles, other frogs, insects and scorpions.

Fertilised eggs hatch in two days and develop into frogs after about 18 days. The young frogs are as ravenous as the adults and will even become cannibalistic. It is a race against time, for as soon as the pools dry up, the bullfrogs must retreat into the ground. Here, they encase themselves in a cocoon of mud, and shut down all but essential services as they pass into a prolonged state of dormancy, known as aestivation. They remain buried until the next thunderstorm, which may be a year or more in coming.

Tortoises are seen only during the rainy season. Two species occur — the small Kalahari tortoise (*Psammobates oculifer*) and the ubiquitous and much larger leopard or mountain tortoise (*Geochelone pardalis*). A surprise resident is the Cape terrapin (*Pelomedusa subrufa*). During dry times tortoises creep into a sheltered place and aestivate, terrapins doing so underground like the bullfrogs. When it rains, the Kalahari tortoise raises itself up on its back legs with its head held down and proceeds to lick the moisture running down its carapace.

The most striking snake in the Kalahari is the highly poisonous but relatively docile Cape cobra (*Naja nivea*). The Kalahari form of this species is a beautiful deep yellow colour, making it conspicuous among the red sand dunes. Some Cape cobras are also peppered with a number of black spots. Puff adders (*Bitis arietans arietans*), the small horned adder (*Bitis caudalis*), mole snakes (*Pseudaspis cana*) and an assortment of sand snakes (*Psammophis* species), make up the rest of the little known Kalahari snake community.

Like most arid areas, the Kalahari has a large and diverse lizard population with 18 species recorded in the park. One of the most characteristic evening sounds in the early summer is the chorus of the barking geckos. As sunset approaches, thousands of these little lizards move to the entrances of their burrows and start calling; a descending and rapid *tjik...tjik...tjik...tjik...tjik...tjik*, like someone knocking two stones together. They use the entrances to their holes to relay the sound. Around sunset and on moonlit nights the barking gecko chorus dominates all else. The scientific name for these noisy little animals is, rather aptly, *Ptenopus garrulus*.

Many Kalahari lizards depend on the same food source — termites. This causes problems of co-existence, which the lizards have largely overcome by a clear breakdown in habitat use and activity schedules. Thus, one lizard may be diurnal and arboreal (living in trees); another may be diurnal but ground-dwelling; and a third nocturnal and arboreal. Each one therefore tends to be active at the time when, and in an area where, the others are not.

An exciting lizard story from the Kalahari is the first substantiated instance of a vertebrate mimicking an invertebrate. Mimicry is an old trick in nature and is the phenomenon in which a palatable or unprotected species (the mimic), has evolved to resemble an unpalatable or protected one (the model). Thus, the mimic deceives potential predators into believing that it is the model, and therefore lessens its chances of being attacked. In this case, the mimic is the juvenile form of a common lizard, known as the black and yellow sand lizard (*Heliobolus lugubris*), and the model is a carabid beetle, colloquially known as the *oogpister*.

Oogpister, euphemistically translated, means eye-squirter, the name being derived from their habit of spraying a pungent acidic fluid when molested. These black beetles have a prominent white stripe around their bodies which acts as a warning colouration to any would-be attacker. Juvenile black and yellow sand lizards are jet black, with a white stripe, and move around with their backs arched in a most un-lizard-like — but beetle-like — manner. A predator encountering a juvenile black and yellow sand lizard might mistake it, at least momentarily, for an *oogpister*. Fearful of receiving an eyeful, it may hesitate to attack and give the young lizard a chance to escape. The adults are duller and more concealingly coloured and move with a typical lizard gait.

Invertebrates

INVERTEBRATES — animals without backbones — are far more numerous than vertebrates. Insects alone account for a staggering 70 per cent of all animal species. The invertebrate fauna of the Kalahari has not been well studied and I can only offer some general notes on a few of these most interesting and important animals.

Termites are one of the oldest insect orders. They have been around for nearly 100 million years, and they have evolved an amazingly complex social life with hundreds of thousands of individuals living and working together in a single colony. A clear division of labour exists between workers, soldiers and sexed individuals. When conditions are propitious, the sexed termites erupt in thousands from their nest as winged nymphs and attempt to start new colonies.

The most commonly seen termites in the Kalahari are harvester termites (*Hodotermes mossambicus*). Unlike most termites, this species does not build a nest mound above the ground. The position of the nest is only revealed by a series of small entrance holes which, if the termites are active, have accumulations of pieces of grass, which have been cut and carried to the entrance by the workers and are ready to be transported underground. The workers of this species are unique among termites in that they have horny, pigmented skins so that they can withstand the sun and forage during the day. For termites, they are also unusual in that they have eyes.

The termite mounds one sees on the plains bordering the Nossob riverbed belong to the snouted harvester termite (*Trinervitermes trinervoides*). This name is derived from the soldiers' heads, which are drawn out in front into a pointed snout. Unlike soldiers of other species, snouted termite soldiers do not have large jaws. They rely instead on chemical warfare to fight their enemies, which include ants and aardwolves. The swollen head of the soldier has a large gland which produces an irritant fluid which it squirts through a pore at the tip of its snout when attacked.

If the fluid gets onto the legs or antennae of an ant, the ant will writhe as though in pain and abandon the fight. Against an aardwolf the amount of irritant fluid produced by a single worker is negligible. But as soon as an aardwolf starts feeding on a patch of foraging workers, those that can escape rush back to the mound, while soldiers quickly come out and converge on the battleground. When the ratio of workers to soldiers reaches a certain level, the aardwolf abandons the food patch. Presumably, the number of soldiers and, therefore, the concentration of irritant fluids builds up to a level unpalatable to the aardwolf.

Beetles are the largest order in the animal kingdom. So far, some 300 000 species have been described worldwide and there are many more to come.

Large and conspicuous dung beetles, which belong to the huge family Scarabaeidae, are common in the Kalahari. Their ability to find fresh dung is incredible. Sometimes, before an animal has even finished defaecating, the first beetles have arrived and are busy rolling away the first dung balls. These are buried close by and provide food for the beetles and their larvae.

Tenebrionid beetles are well adapted to arid areas. Perhaps the best known of this large family are the *toktokkie* beetles. Large beetles which have lost their wings, they are named for their habit of knocking on the ground loudly at intervals, apparently in order to attract the opposite sex. The tapping sound is produced by raising the abdomen and bringing it down on the ground rapidly, several times in succession.

A group of comparatively small beetles, with enlarged hind legs enabling them to jump well and so avoid predation, are known as flea beetles belonging to the sub-family Halticinae. Flea beetles are of interest as several species are the source of Bushman arrow poison. The larvae of each species of flea beetle feed on the leaves of a particular species of host tree and, when mature, drop off and burrow some 50 to 100 cm into the ground. Here the larvae of another beetle, belonging to the genus *Lebistina*, parasitise the flea beetle larvae. The Bushmen believe that the *Lebistina* larvae produce a more effective poison than the host larvae.

The parasites attach themselves to the flea beetle larvae, penetrating their hard-walled cocoons. The Bushmen dig up the cocoons, knowing where to do so because of the attachment of each species of flea beetle larvae to a certain tree species. They then carefully open the cocoons, extract the pupae and squeeze the body juices onto the shaft of an arrow. So deadly is this poison that a well placed arrow will kill a full-grown giraffe in 30 minutes.

Better known among the poisonous animals of the Kalahari are the scorpions. The two most important scorpion families are the Scorpionidae and the Buthidae. With their large pincers, the Scorpionidae look particularly dangerous. However, they have slender tails with a small sting and it is the small-pincered, large-stinged Buthidae that are more poisonous. There are some Buthidae whose stings can be fatal to some humans, particularly children. Scorpions are mainly nocturnal and seem to be most active on windy nights. Under such conditions, it is unwise to walk without shoes on.

In spite of being so dangerous, scorpions do appear to be good eating and are preyed upon by a wide range of mammals and birds. Their young are born live and, except for size, resemble the adults. The mother carries her dozens of young around on her back. An indication of how resilient and well adapted to desert conditions scorpions are can be gleaned from the fact that certain species have been kept in a laboratory for more than a year without food or water.

Worthy of respect but not dangerous are the millipedes. The Kalahari produces millipedes as big as can be found anywhere. Commonly known as a *duisendpoot* (thousand feet), these long, cylindrical, many-jointed vegetarian arthropods are seen only after rain, when they emerge from underground burrows. When handled they eject a defensive, repulsive fluid which contains cyanide. This can lead to purplish black sores and sloughing of the skin from sensitive spots such as under the fingernails.

Their reproduction is curious: fertilisation takes place at the front end. Both sexes have paired genital openings on the third segment. In addition, the male's legs, on the seventh segment, are modified into organs called gonopods. Before copulation, he charges his gonopods with sperm from his own genital openings and inserts the gonopods into the female genital opening to effect transfer of the sperm. To do this, the male and female contort around each other, or the male rides in tandem on the back of the female. Sometimes, tripledeckers — two males above one female — may be seen gliding around.

After this the record becomes hazy. It is not known how long the eggs take to develop and one rarely sees very small individuals. Whether this is due to the rapid development or very secretive habits of the young is unknown. The preponderance of adults could also reflect that millipedes have a long adult life.

The Guinness Book of Records gives the world record length of a millipede jointly to individuals of two species — one from East Africa and one from the Seychelles — each with a length of 280 mm. I would not be surprised if a Kalahari king millipede could beat this record.

CHAPTER NINE

Getting the most out of your visit

THE Kalahari Gemsbok National Park is not the easiest place in the world to get to. This may be a blessing as it is only the committed nature lover who is prepared to undertake the long and arduous journey.

For those who can afford it, it is possible to fly into the park and hire a vehicle once there. This must be by prior arrangement with the park warden. It is also possible to fly to Upington and hire a car and a guide through the Upington municipality.

Routes and accommodation

THE majority of visitors prefer to travel in their own cars. Upington (from the south) and Kuruman (from the east) are the two main gateways to the park through South Africa. From Namibia the park can be approached from Keetmanshoop (from the south) or Mariental (from the north). All these approaches involve travel over more than 300 km of gravel roads, although the road from Upington is due to be tarred soon, as are the roads in the park.

The condition of these roads varies, depending largely on when they were last graded. Tyres should be deflated 0,4–0,6 bars when driving on gravel roads for more comfortable travelling. The only time that the roads become impassable is during heavy rains when one or other of the rivers comes down in flood. Any modern car in good condition should make the journey without any trouble as long as it is not overloaded, but I do not recommend towing a caravan to the park.

For those with a reliable four-wheel-drive vehicle and a spirit of adventure, the Mabua Sehube area in the Gemsbok National Park offers excitement and challenge. Mabua Sehube Pan is on the main road from Tshabong to Hukuntsi, but the road is bad and there are no facilities in the reserve, not even a reliable water supply.

Johannesburg to Twee Rivieren is 920 km. An overnight stop at Kuruman (540 km from Johannesburg) gives the traveller time to visit the Eye and the Moffat Mission Church with the tree under which Livingstone proposed to Moffat's daughter. The gravel begins at Hotazel and the only hotels between here and Twee Rivieren are at Vanzylsrus, 220 km from Twee Rivieren, and the Molopo Motel, 58 km from Twee Rivieren. However, a convenient camping site with clean showers and firewood has recently been opened near Askham, 110 km from Vanzylsrus.

From Cape Town the park access route is via Upington, 880 km from the mother city. There are three hotels in Upington and a caravan park with modern chalets for hire at a place called "Die Eiland" run by the municipality. There are two routes from Upington to Twee Rivieren. The recommended one is via Noenieput along the Molopo riverbed, a distance of 308 km. An alternative route, shorter by 40 km, is over the dunes along the Theuns van der Westhuizen road. This road is usually no worse than the Noenieput road and is an interesting drive through the dunes and across some large pans. Take a good map as there are several unmarked turn-offs along the way.

From Namibia you enter the Kalahari Gemsbok National Park at Mata Mata, 312 km on gravel from Keetmanshoop, or 344 km from Mariental.

Accommodation and camping in the park are provided at three small rest camps: Twee Rivieren, Mata Mata and Nossob. All accommodation includes cutlery and crockery, bedding, soap and towels. Huts with kitchenettes and fridges, showers and toilets, and huts where these facilities are shared (Nossob and Mata Mata only) are provided.

At Twee Rivieren the huts are air conditioned while the power is on, from about 05h00 to 22h00, and there is a small swimming pool in which to cool off. There is no air conditioning at Nossob or Mata Mata, and electrical power is provided only from half an hour before the gates open until 10h00 and again from 18h00 until 22h00. Nossob has a large area of natural vegetation within the camp where visitors can examine it closely. Nossob also has a small information centre which provides some basic background on the ecology of the Kalahari. At present this is the only information facility in the park and no regular film shows or talks are given at any of the camps.

Camp grounds with ablution blocks as well as facilities for washing clothes are also provided at all three camps. At each rest camp a shop sells basic provisions, but no bread, fresh vegetables or film. Fresh meat and eggs are on sale only at Twee Rivieren, which is also the only camp to have a restaurant, serving brunch (10h00-11h00) and an evening braai.

Tips for travel in the park

DISTANCES between the camps are large: 160 km from Twee Rivieren to Nossob and Nossob to Mata Mata, and 130 km from Twee Rivieren to Mata Mata. Visitors leaving Twee Rivieren or Mata Mata for Nossob, or vice versa, must do so before noon. All cars leaving a rest camp are noted and any missing cars are looked for that night. It is advisable to take drinking water with you and in winter something warm to wear, just in case. If you do have a breakdown, stay in your car. Someone will rescue you before too long. The worst thing to do is to leave your car and walk.

The two most common problems encountered by tourists with vehicles are getting stuck in the sand, and having the radiator freeze in winter. If you do get stuck in a sandy patch, do not try to force the vehicle out. Stop the car immediately, have a good look around for any danger, then alight from your vehicle and deflate the tyres anything up to 1,0 bar, or for 10-20 seconds. Ask passengers to help by pushing as you try and drive the car out — but do not rev the engine so much that the wheels start spinning, as this will only cause the vehicle to dig deeper into the sand. If you are successful you will have to reinflate your tyres when you get to the next camp, but remember to keep them slightly lower than the recommended pressure, as this makes for more comfortable travel over corrugations and better traction in sand. As long as you travel slowly, the lowered pressure will do your tyres no harm.

TABLE 2
Hours of travel in the Kalahari Gemsbok National Park

MONTH	GATES OPEN	GATES CLOSE
January	06h00	19h30
February	06h30	19h30
March	06h30	19h00
April	07h00	18h30
May	07h00	18h00
June/July	07h30	18h00
August	07h00	18h30
September	06h30	18h30
October	06h00	19h00
November/		
December	05h30	19h30

Note: Shops and offices are open from the time the gates open to half an hour after closing time.

Although most cars today have an anti-freeze mixture in their radiators, the radiator water may still freeze overnight during a particularly cold snap. When this happens the engine overheats very soon after being started. The only thing to do is to switch off the engine immediately and wait for the ice to thaw. To help prevent the radiator water from freezing in the first place, a few precautions should be taken; never park the car pointing south as this is the direction from which the cold wind blows, and remember that an old blanket or tarpaulin to cover the radiator goes a long way in preventing freezing.

Five picnic places (one in the Auob riverbed and four in the Nossob) are situated between camps. At each, stone tables and chairs, basic toilet facilities and firewood are provided. These picnic areas used to be fenced, but after lions chased a gemsbok through the fence at Kamqua and killed it in the enclosed area, the fences were removed. A sociable weaver nest at Kamqua provides a good opportunity for observing and photographing these birds at close quarters. I have also known pygmy falcons to occupy this nest. The picnic areas are also good places to observe and photograph rodents, even ground squirrels, and other small birds which are attracted by the food scraps.

For the traveller including a stop over in the Kalahari Gemsbok National Park as part of a general tour of the northern Cape and/or Namibia, at least three nights in the park are required to do it justice. Spend the first night at one of the two entrance gate camps, Twee Rivieren or Mata Mata, depending on where you are coming from, one at Nossob and then the final night at the other entrance gate. Include a trip over the dunes road from Kamqua to Kameelsleep. Although you probably will not see as much game on this road as along the riverbeds, it gives you a good idea of what the extensive dune areas of the Kalahari look like. If you are prone to car sickness, however, be careful on this road as the up and down motion over the dunes may lead to an uncomfortable journey!

For those who can spend longer in the park it is a good idea to spend at least two nights at Nossob so that a "pilgrimage" to Union's End, 130 km north of Nossob camp, can be made. After this I would suggest spending more or less equal periods of time at each camp. However, because of the unpredictability of game movements, you may find that you want to stay longer at one camp than another. Although it is often impossible to change your booking during the busy times such as school holidays, it is usually possible to do so during the quieter times. The tourist officers will always try to help.

Game viewing strategies

THE Kalahari is rewarding for the keen photographer. The openness of the area makes it easier to photograph animals than in lush country where vegetation often obscures the subject. The lack of cloud cover provides ideal lighting, particularly in the early morning and late afternoon, and sunsets, especially in summer, can be stunningly beautiful. But be careful when the sun gets up a bit: the harsh light and reflective surfaces, particularly along the riverbeds, make it very easy to overexpose your shots. Both long and wide angle lenses will be used, so be sure to take all your lenses.

Sitting and waiting at a windmill is a good strategy for viewing and photographing birds and mammals. Cubitje Quap near Nossob, Melkvlei near Twee Rivieren and the Groot and Klein Skrijs in the northern Auob are some of my favourite spots. But the situation varies, different watering points attract animals at different times, and you should look around a bit first when coming into a new area. Most animals prefer the sweet water of windmills such as Rooiputs, Cubitje Quap, Kwang and Kannaguass in the Nossob and most of those in the Auob. However, gemsbok often visit the salty windmills such as Melkvlei, Jan se Draai, Kaspersdraai, Groot Brak, Leijersdraai and Groot Kolk.

Several of the windmills have provided drama and adventure to Kalahari inhabitants over the years. As indicated in chapter 1, Groot Kolk was the scene of a massacre of German troops by Hottentots during the so-called Hottentot Rebellion. At Groot Brak the German geologist Hans Schwabe met his end and his body was partially eaten by spotted hyaenas. Gemsbokplein was the home of the first wardens of the Kalahari Gemsbok National Park.

On a personal level several incidents at windmills stick in my mind. Early one evening not long after we had arrived in the Kalahari, Margie and I got stuck in the mud at Kaspersdraai after a severe rainstorm. In order to get out of the mud we needed to jack up the car and place some logs under the wheels. By the time we had worked this out it was dark and the nearest logs were about 100 metres away. I wanted to walk over to them, but my wife of two months was dead against it. We had a spotlight on the vehicle and after a thorough search for any danger I decided to go and get the logs in spite of Margie's strong protests.

She of course had to shine the spotlight, and I had gone barely 20 metres when she shouted, "Gus there's a lion coming towards you!" Sure enough, in the spotlight beam I saw a pair of shining eyes approaching me. I retreated rapidly to the car to a very irate and upset wife. Even after discovering that the lion was actually a spotted hyaena I did not have the courage to attempt the excursion again, and we spent a very long three hours waiting in stony silence until we were rescued.

I often used to spend nights at windmills when on field expeditions. If I was alone I slept on the back of my truck. I usually pulled up close to the drinking trough in the hope of hearing any animals, particularly marked hyaenas I was looking for, that might come and drink during the night. One night at Kannaguass I was awakened by the sound of lapping. I switched on the spotlight and was greeted by the thrilling sight of 11 lions not 10 metres away, packed tightly together at the pool. They must have spent five minutes there showing absolutely no concern for the spotlight or my presence.

When Margie and I first started trying to follow hyaenas at night we were not very successful, spending most of the night following a radio signal and getting only occasional fleeting glimpses of the hyaenas. We were simply not proficient enough at driving over the dunes in darkness. We had spent two frustrating and exhausting nights trying to keep contact with a brown hyaena called Harken when he came to Rooikop

windmill. When we caught up with him we found him standing eyeball to eyeball with an unknown male.

The two brown hyaenas broke into a fierce but highly ritualised territorial battle, which was accompanied by the most marvellous growls, snarls and yells. We watched spellbound as the two animals wrestled in our spotlight, seemingly oblivious to our presence. Our hyaena lost the encounter and was chased back into the dunes by the victor, leaving us following radio signals again until daylight. It was incidents like this that encouraged us to persevere with trying to follow hyaenas until we got it right and were able to keep them in visual contact most of the time. For months afterwards we could not pass Rooikop without recalling that exciting battle.

Because of the comparatively low density of animals in the Kalahari and their habit of moving large distances, driving around slowly looking for animals is often more rewarding than waiting around at a windmill. On balance I would recommend splitting your time to 75 per cent driving around and 25 per cent sitting and waiting.

It is advisable to get out of camp as early as possible in the morning, particularly in summer. Most predators are predominantly nocturnal and so the best time to look for them is early morning and late afternoon. At these times of day you should drive around slowly, paying attention to the behaviour of antelope. Any buck standing still and looking intently in one direction may well have spotted a predator and it is a good idea to stop and scan the surroundings. Remember too, that two or three chanting goshawks in a tree or on a bush usually mean there's a honey badger at hand. Doves come to water at sunrise and sunset in summer and sandgrouse arrive later in the morning.

In winter, especially if there have been good summer rains, seed-eating birds will be coming and going to water throughout the day. And if they are around, so will small raptors like gabar goshawks and rednecked falcons. By 09h00 to 10h00 in summer most of the animals will be resting in the shade and there is little point in driving around in the heat. If possible return to camp, or rest up at a picnic area until about 16h00 when the animals will slowly start to become active again. In winter, however, it is more worthwhile being about all day.

When trying to rest in the heat of the day with no air conditioning, strip the bed down to the sheets, take a cold shower, and, without drying yourself, lie on your damp towel. An advantage of the Kalahari heat is that it is usually dry and cools down at night, when it is very pleasant to sleep on the stoep of your hut. Keep the windows and doors of your hut open at night to let in as much cool air as possible, but close up and draw the curtains during the day to keep the hot air out.

When to visit the park

WHEN is the best time to visit the Kalahari? The Kalahari is undoubtedly at its most spectacular after good rains — this is usually in March-April in years of high rainfall. Then large concentrations of game collect along the riverbeds and

TABLE 3
Average monthly rainfall and minimum and maximum temperatures at Twee Rivieren

MONTH	RAINFALL (mm)	MIN TEMP (°C)	MAX TEMP (°C)
January	48,7	19,6	35,5
February	41,5	18,5	34,9
March	30,9	16,8	32,5
April	35,0	11,6	28,5
May	13,4	5,5	22,9
June	4,1	2,2	21,5
July	1,0	1,1	21,8
August	1,0	2,7	23,8
September	0,6	7,3	28,7
October	11,6	11,8	30,9
November	18,3	15,9	33,5
December	14,3	17,9	33,1
TOTAL	220,3		

around pans, the annual plants burst into bloom and raptors collect in spectacular numbers at termite eruptions. During the winter the concentrations of game usually break up, except in certain years during a dry cycle when spectacular winter influxes may occur. However, the riverbeds are still full of activity and although the nights are cold, the days are usually glorious.

Early summer is good for canids as they can often be seen at dens along the riverbeds, giving unrivalled opportunities for observing and photographing jackals and foxes, but this is often a very dry time with few ungulates to be found along the riverbeds. In December and January the springbok usually drop their lambs, providing beauty and drama (there are often predators close by) to those who don't mind the heat.

So each season has its fascination

and character and the serious Kalahari enthusiast should experience
them all.

During times when there are fewer
animals to be seen, detailed observations of the behaviour of those that
are around often provide more enjoy-
ment and fulfilment than hurrying
along through large concentrations
of game.

Checklist of birds

KEY:

V = Vagrant   (152 species)   Irregular visitors, may be common in some years
M = Migrant   (16 species)   Regular, seasonal visitor
R = Resident   (78 species)   Always present
N = Nomad   (18 species)   Regular, but unseasonal visitor

(Standard southern African bird numbers, as used in *Roberts' Birds of Southern Africa* and *Newman's Birds of Southern Africa*, are given with the common names.)

Struthio camelus	1 Ostrich (R)
Tachybaptus ruficollis	8 Dabchick (V)
Pelecanus rufescens	50 Pinkbacked pelican (V)
Phalacrocorax carbo	55 Whitebreasted cormorant (V)
Phalacrocorax africanus	58 Reed cormorant (V)
Ardea cinerea	62 Grey heron (V)
Ardea melanocephala	63 Blackheaded heron (V)
Ardea purpurea	65 Purple heron (V)
Egretta alba	66 Great white egret (V)
Egretta garzetta	67 Little egret (V)
Egretta intermedia	68 Yellowbilled egret (V)
Bubulcus ibis	71 Cattle egret (V)
Ardeola ralloides	72 Squacco heron (V)
Nycticorax nycticorax	76 Blackcrowned night heron (V)
Ixobrychus minutus	78 Little bittern (V)
Ixobrychus sturmii	79 Dwarf bittern (V)
Scopus umbretta	81 Hamerkop (V)
Ciconia ciconia	83 White stork (V)
Ciconia nigra	84 Black stork (V)
Ciconia abdimii	85 Abdim's stork (V)
Ciconia episcopus	86 Woollynecked stork (V)
Ephippiorhynchus senegalensis	88 Saddlebilled stork (V)
Leptoptilos crumeniferus	89 Marabou stork (V)
Mycteria ibis	90 Yellowbilled stork (V)
Threskiornis aethiopicus	91 Sacred ibis (V)
Plegadis falcinellus	93 Glossy ibis (V)
Platalea alba	95 African spoonbill (V)
Phoenicopterus minor	97 Lesser flamingo (V)
Dendrocygna viduata	99 Whitefaced duck (V)
Thalassornis leuconotus	101 Whitebacked duck (V)
Alopochen aegyptiacus	102 Egyptian goose (V)
Tadorna cana	103 South African shelduck (V)
Anas undulata	104 Yellowbilled duck (V)
Anas erythrorhyncha	108 Redbilled teal (V)
Anas smithii	112 Cape shoveller (V)
Netta erythrophthalma	113 Southern pochard (V)
Sarkidiornis melanotos	115 Knobbilled duck (V)
Plectropterus gambensis	116 Spurwinged goose (V)
Sagittarius serpentarius	118 Secretarybird (R)
Necrosyrtes monachus	121 Hooded vulture (V)
Gyps coprotheres	122 Cape Vulture (V)
Gyps africanus	123 Whitebacked vulture (R)

Torgos tracheliotus	124 Lappetfaced vulture (R)
Trigonoceps occipitalis	125 Whiteheaded vulture (V)
Milvus migrans migrans	126 Black kite (M)
Milvus migrans parasitus	126 Yellowbilled kite (M)
Elanus caeruleus	127 Blackshouldered kite (R)
Aquila verreauxii	131 Black eagle (V)
Aquila rapax	132 Tawny eagle (R)
Aquila nipalensis	133 Steppe eagle (M)
Aquila wahlbergi	135 Wahlberg's eagle (V)
Hieraaetus pennatus	136 Booted eagle (M)
Hieraaetus fasciatus	137 African hawk eagle (V)
Polemaetus bellicosus	140 Martial eagle (R)
Circaetus cinereus	142 Brown snake eagle (R)
Circaetus gallicus	143 Blackbreasted snake eagle (R)
Terathopius ecaudatus	146 Bateleur (R)
Gypohierax angolensis	147 Palmnut vulture (V)
Haliaeetus vocifer	148 Fish eagle (V)
Buteo buteo	149 Steppe buzzard (V)
Buteo rufofuscus	152 Jackal buzzard (V)
Accipiter ovampensis	156 Ovambo sparrowhawk (V)
Accipiter minullus	157 Little sparrowhawk (V)
Accipiter badius	159 Little banded goshawk (V)
Micronisus gabar	161 Gabar goshawk (R)
Melierax canorus	162 Pale chanting goshawk (R)
Circus pygargus	166 Montagu's harrier (V)
Circus macrourus	167 Pallid harrier (V)
Circus maurus	168 Black harrier (V)
Polyboroides typus	169 Gymnogene (V)
Falco biarmicus	172 Lanner (R)
Falco subbuteo	173 Hobby (V)
Falco concolor	175 Sooty falcon (V)
Falco chicquera	178 Rednecked falcon (R)
Falco vespertinus	179 Western redfooted kestrel (M)
Falco amurensis	180 Eastern redfooted kestrel (V)
Falco tinnunculus	181 Rock kestrel (R)
Falco rupicoloides	182 Greater kestrel (R)
Falco naumanni	183 Lesser kestrel (V)
Falco dickinsoni	185 Dickinson's kestrel (V)
Polihierax semitorquatus	186 Pygmy falcon (R)
Francolinus adspersus	194 Redbilled francolin (V)
Coturnix coturnix	200 Common quail (N)
Coturnix delegorguei	201 Harlequin quail (V)
Numida meleagris	203 Helmeted guineafowl (V)
Turnix sylvatica	205 Kurrichane buttonquail (N)
Crex egregia	212 African crake (V)
Porzana porzana	214 Spotted crake (V)
Sarothrura elegans	218 Buffspotted flufftail (V)
Porphyrio porphyrio	223 Purple gallinule (V)
Gallinula angulata	227 Lesser moorhen (V)
Fulica cristata	228 Redknobbed coot (V)
Ardeotis kori	230 Kori bustard (R)
Neotis denhami	231 Stanley's bustard (V)
Neotis ludwiggii	232 Ludwig's bustard (V)
Eupodotis ruficrista	237 Redcrested korhaan (R)
Eupodotis afra	239 Black korhaan (R)
Actophilornis africanus	240 African jacana (V)
Rostratula benghalensis	242 Painted snipe (V)
Charadrius marginatus	246 Whitefronted plover (V)
Charadrius tricollaris	249 Threebanded plover (V)
Charadrius asiaticus	252 Caspian plover (V)
Pluvialis squatarola	254 Grey plover (V)
Vanellus coronatus	255 Crowned plover (R)

Vanellus armatus
Arenaria interpes
Tringa hypoleucos
Tringa glareola
Tringa stagnatilis
Tringa nebularia
Calidris ferruginea
Calidris minuta
Philomachus pugnax
Numenius phaeopus
Recurvirostra avosetta
Himantopus himantopus
Burhinus capensis
Cursorius rufus
Cursorius temminckii
Rhinoptilus africanus
Rhinoptilus chalcopterus
Glareola nordmanni
Stercorarius longicaudus
Chlidonias leucopterus
Pterocles namaqua
Pterocles burchelli
Columba guinea
Streptopelia capicola
Streptopelia senegalensis
Oena capensis
Agapornis roseicollis
Cuculus canorus
Clamator glandarius
Clamator jacobinus
Chrysococcyx caprius
Tyto alba
Tyto capensis
Otus senegalensis
Otus leucotis
Glaucidium perlatum
Bubo africanus
Bubo lacteus
Caprimulgus europaeus
Caprimulgus rufigena
Apus apus
Apus barbatus
Apus caffer
Apus affinis
Colius colius
Colius indicus
Halcyon chelicuti
Merops apiaster
Merops hirundineus
Coracias garrulus
Coracias caudata
Coracias naevia
Upupa epops
Phoeniculus purpureus
Phoeniculus cyanomelas
Tockus nasutus
Tockus flavirostris
Lybius leucomelas
Dendropicos fuscescens
Thripias namaquus
Mirafra passerina
Mirafra apiata

258 Blacksmith plover (V)
262 Turnstone (V)
263 Common sandpiper (M)
266 Wood sandpiper (M)
269 Marsh sandpiper (V)
270 Greenshank (M)
272 Curlew sandpiper (V)
274 Little stint (V)
284 Ruff (V)
290 Whimbrel (V)
294 Avocet (V)
295 Blackwinged stilt (V)
297 Spotted dikkop (R)
299 Burchell's courser (N)
300 Temminck's courser (V)
301 Doublebanded courser (R)
303 Bronzewinged courser (V)
305 Blackwinged pratincole (V)
308 Longtailed skua (V)
339 Whitewinged tern (V)
344 Namaqua sandgrouse (R)
345 Burchell's sandgrouse (R)
349 Rock pigeon (V)
354 Cape turtle dove (R)
355 Laughing dove (R)
356 Namaqua dove (R)
367 Rosyfaced lovebird (V)
374 European cuckoo (V)
380 Great spotted cuckoo (V)
382 Jacobin cuckoo (V)
386 Diederik cuckoo (M)
392 Barn owl (R)
393 Grass owl (V)
396 Scops owl (R)
397 Whitefaced owl (R)
398 Pearlspotted owl (R)
401 Spotted eagle owl (R)
402 Giant eagle owl (R)
404 European nightjar (V)
406 Rufoucheeked nightjar (M)
411 European swift (M)
412 Black swift (M)
415 Whiterumped swift (V)
417 Little swift (V)
425 Whitebacked mousebird (V)
426 Redfaced mousebird (V)
437 Striped kingfisher (V)
438 European bee-eater (V)
445 Swallowtailed bee-eater (R)
446 European roller (V)
447 Lilacbreasted roller (R)
449 Purple roller (M)
451 Hoopoe (R)
452 Redbilled woodhoopoe (V)
454 Scimitarbilled woodhoopoe (R)
457 Grey hornbill (V)
459 Yellowbilled hornbill (R)
465 Pied barbet (R)
486 Cardinal woodpecker (R)
487 Bearded woodpecker (V)
493 Monotonous lark (V)
495 Clapper lark (R)

Mirafra africanoides	497 Fawncoloured lark (R)
Mirafra sabota	498 Sabota lark (R)
Pinarocorys nigricans	505 Dusky lark (V)
Chersomanes albofasciata	506 Spikeheeled lark (R)
Calandrella cinerea	507 Redcapped lark (N)
Calandrella conirostris	508 Pinkbilled lark (N)
Spizocorys sclateri	510 Sclater's lark (N)
Alauda starki	511 Stark's lark (N)
Eremopterix leucotis	515 Chestnutbacked finchlark (N)
Eremopterix verticalis	516 Greybacked finchlark (N)
Eremopterix australis	517 Blackeared finchlark (V)
Hirundo rustica	518 European swallow (V)
Hirundo albigularis	520 Whitethroated swallow (V)
Hirundo dimidiata	523 Pearlbreasted swallow (V)
Hirundo culcullata	526 Greater striped swallow (V)
Hirundo abyssinica	527 Lesser striped swallow (V)
Hirundo spilodera	528 South African cliff swallow (R)
Hirundo fuligula	529 Rock martin (R)
Delichon urbica	530 House martin (V)
Riparia paludicola	533 Brownthroated martin (V)
Dicrurus adsimilis	541 Forktailed drongo (R)
Oriolus oriolus	544 European golden oriole (V)
Corvus capensis	547 Black crow (R)
Corvus albus	548 Pied crow (V)
Parus afer	551 Southern grey tit (R)
Anthoscopus minutus	557 Cape penduline tit (R)
Turdoides bicolor	563 Pied babbler (V)
Pycnonotus nigricans	567 Redeyed bulbul (R)
Turdus litsitsirupa	580 Groundscraper thrush (V)
Monticola brevipes	583 Shorttoed rock thrush (V)
Oenanthe monticola	586 Mountain chat (V)
Oenanthe pileata	587 Capped wheatear (M)
Cercomela familiaris	589 Familiar chat (R)
Cercomela tractrac	590 Tractrac chat (V)
Cercomela schlegelii	592 Karoo chat (V)
Myrmecocichla formicivora	595 Anteating chat (R)
Erythropygia paena	615 Kalahari robin (R)
Parisome subcaeruleum	621 Titbabbler (R)
Acrocephalus schoenobaenus	634 European sedge warbler (V)
Phylloscopus trochilus	643 Willow warbler (V)
Sylvietta rufescens	651 Longbilled crombec (V)
Eremomela icteropygialis	653 Yellowbellied eremomela (R)
Cisticola juncidis	664 Fantailed cisticola (N)
Cisticola aridula	665 Desert cisticola (R)
Cisticola fulvicapilla	681 Neddicky (V)
Prinia flavicans	685 Blackchested prinia (R)
Malcorus pectoralis	688 Rufouseared warbler (R)
Muscicapa striata	689 Spotted flycatcher (V)
Melaenornis mariquensis	695 Marico flycatcher (R)
Melaenornis infuscatus	697 Chat flycatcher (R)
Batis pririt	703 Pririt batis (R)
Terpsiphone viridis	710 Paradise flycatcher (V)
Motacilla capensis	713 Cape wagtail (V)
Motacilla cinerea	715 Grey wagtail (V)
Anthus novaeseelandiae	716 Richard's pipit (N)
Anthus similis	717 Longbilled pipit (N)
Anthus vaalensis	719 Buffy pipit (N)
Lanius minor	731 Lesser grey shrike (M)
Lanius collaris	732 Fiscal shrike (R)
Lanius collurio	733 Redbacked shrike (M)
Laniarius atrococcineus	739 Crimsonbreasted shrike (R)
Nilaus afer	741 Brubru (R)

Tchagra australis
Telophorus zeylonus
Eurocephalus anguitimens
Spreo bicolor
Creatophora cinerea
Cinnyricinclus leucogaster
Lamprotornis australis
Lamprotornis nitens
Nectarinia mariquensis
Nectarinia fusca
Zosterops pallidus
Bubalornis niger
Plocepasser mahali
Philetairus socius
Passer domesticus
Passer motitensis
Passer melanurus
Passer griseus
Sporopipes squamifrons
Ploceus velatus
Quelea quelea
Euplectes orix
Euplectes afer
Pytilia melba
Lagonosticta senegala
Uraeginthus granatinus
Estrilda astrild
Estrilda erythronotos
Amadina erythrocephala
Vidua regia
Serinus atrogularis
Serinus alario
Serinus flaviventris
Emberiza flaviventris
Emberiza tahapisi
Emberiza impetuani

743 Threestreaked tchagra (V)
746 Bokmakierie (R)
756 Whitecrowned shrike (V)
759 Pied starling (V)
760 Wattled starling (N)
761 Plumcoloured starling (V)
762 Burchell's starling (R)
764 Glossy starling (R)
779 Marico sunbird (V)
788 Dusky sunbird (V)
796 Cape white-eye (V)
798 Redbilled buffalo weaver (V)
799 Whitebrowed sparrowweaver (R)
800 Sociable weaver (R)
801 House sparrow (R)
802 Great sparrow (N)
803 Cape sparrow (R)
804 Greyheaded sparrow (R)
806 Scalyfeathered finch (R)
814 Masked weaver (R)
821 Redbilled quelea (N)
824 Red bishop (V)
826 Golden bishop (V)
834 Melba finch (V)
842 Redbilled firefinch (V)
845 Violeteared waxbill (V)
846 Common waxbill (V)
847 Blackcheeked waxbill (V)
856 Redheaded finch (N)
861 Shafttailed whydah (R)
870 Blackthroated canary (V)
876 Blackheaded canary (V)
878 Yellow canary (R)
884 Goldenbreasted bunting (V)
886 Rock bunting (V)
887 Larklike bunting (N)

Checklist of mammals

KEY:

1. Very rare
2. Rare
3. Fairly common
4. Common
5. Abundant

(Nomenclature after Smithers, R.H.N. (1983) *The mammals of the southern African subregion*, Pretoria: University of Pretoria.)

ORDER: INSECTIVORA
Crocidura hirta deserti — Desert musk shrew (1)
Erinaceus frontalis — Hedgehog (1)
Chrysochloris asiatica — Cape golden mole (1)
Macroscelides proboscideus — Round-eared elephant-shrew (1)
Elephantulus intufi — Bushveld elephant-shrew (3)

ORDER: CHIROPTERA
Tadarida aegyptiaca bocagei — Egyptian free-tailed bat (2)
Eptesicus capensis — Cape serotine bat (2)
Scotophilus dinganii — Yellow house bat (1)
Nycteris thebaica — Common slit-faced bat (2)

ORDER: PRIMATES
Papio ursinus — Chacma baboon (1)

ORDER: PHOLIDOTA
Manis temminckii — Pangolin (1)

ORDER: LAGOMORPHA
Lepus capensis — Cape hare (4)
Lepus saxatilis — Scrub hare (2)

ORDER: RODENTIA
Cryptomys hottentotus damarensis — Damara molerat (3)
Hystrix africaeaustralis — Porcupine (4)
Pedetes capensis — Springhare (5)
Xerus inauris — Ground squirrel (5)
Parotomys brantsii — Brants' whistling rat (4)
Rhabdomys pumilio — Striped mouse (5)
Zelotomys woosnami — Woosnam's desert rat or tree rat (2)
Mus minutoides — Pygmy mouse (3)
Thallomys paedulcus — Tree mouse (4)
Aethomys namaquensis — Namaqua rock mouse (1)
Saccostomus campestris — Pouched mouse (1)
Malacothrix typica — Large-eared mouse (1)
Dendromus melanotis — Grey climbing mouse (2)
Desmodillus auricularis — Namaqualand or short-tailed gerbil (3)
Gerbillurus paeba — Hairy-footed or pygmy gerbil (5)
Tatera brantsii — Highveld or Brants' gerbil (3)

ORDER: CARNIVORA
Family: Hyaenidae
   Proteles cristatus   Aardwolf (2)
   Hyaena brunnea   Brown hyaena (4)
   Crocuta crocuta   Spotted hyaena (3)
Family: Felidae
   Acinonyx jubatus   Cheetah (3)
   Panthera pardus   Leopard (4)
   Panthera leo   Lion (4)
   Felis caracal   Caracal (3)
   Felis lybica   African wild cat (4)
   Felis nigripes   Small spotted or black-footed cat (1)
Family: Canidae
   Otocyon megalotis   Bat-eared fox (5)
   Lycaon pictus   Wild dog (1)
   Vulpes chama   Cape fox (4)
   Canis mesomelas   Black-backed jackal (5)
Family: Mustelidae
   Mellivora capensis   Honey badger (3)
   Ictonyx striatus   Striped polecat (4)
Family: Viverridae
   Genetta genetta   Small-spotted genet (2)
   Suricata suricatta   Suricate (5)
   Cynictis penicillata   Yellow mongoose (4)
   Galerella sanguinea   Slender mongoose (2)
   Mungos mungo   Banded mongoose (1)

ORDER: TUBULIDENTATA
   Orycteropus afer   Antbear or aardvark (2)

ORDER: ARTIODACTYLA
   Phachochoerus aethiopicus   Warthog (1)
   Connochaetes taurinus   Blue wildebeest (5)
   Alcelaphus buselaphus caama Red hartebeest (5)
   Sylvicapra grimmia   Common duiker (4)
   Antidorcas marsupialis   Springbok (5)
   Raphicerus campestris   Steenbok (5)
   Aepyceros melampus   Impala (1)
   Tragelaphus strepsiceros   Kudu (1)
   Oryx gazella   Gemsbok (5)
   Traurotragus oryx   Eland (3)

List of common plants

(Note: An up to date and complete list of plants collected from the park can be found in: Van Rooyen, N., D.J. van Rensburg, G.K. Theron and J. du P. Bothma, 1988. A checklist of flowering plants of the Kalahari Gemsbok National Park. *Koedoe 31:* 115-135.)

Scientific Name	Common Name	Habitat
Trees and shrubs		
Acacia erioloba	camelthorn/kameeldoring	river and dune
A. erioloba x A. haematoxylon (hibrid)	basterkameel	river
A. haematoxylon	grey camelthorn/vaalkameel	river and dune
A. hebeclada	candle acacia/trassiebos	river and dune
A. luederitzii var. luederitzii	bastard umbrella thorn/swartbas	dune
A. mellifera subsp. detinens	blackthorn/swarthaak	river and dune
Albizia anthelmintica	worm-bark false-thorn/arub	dune
Boscia albitrunca	shepherd's tree/witgat	dune
Crotalaria spartioides	broom/besembos	dune
C. virgultalis	broom/besembos	dune
Galenia africana	kraalbos	river
Grewia flava	brandybush/bessiebos	dune
H. modesta	lusernbos	dune
Hermannia tomentosa	pleisterbossie	dune
Lycium oxycarpum	brosdoring	river
L. hirsutum	wolwedoring	river
Lebeckia linearifolia	bloubos	river
Monechma genistifolium	perdebos	river and dune
M. incanum	bloubos	dune
Rhigozum trichotomum	driedoring	river and dune
Parkinsonia africana	wild green-hair tree/lemoendoring	river
Pentzia incana	karoobossie	river and dune
Plinthus sericeus	sand ganna	river
Salsola rabieana	groot ganna	river and dune
Terminalia sericea	silver cluster-leaf/geelhout	dune
Herbs		
Acanthosicyos naudinianus	gemsbok cucumber	dune
Asparagus spp.	katdoring	river and dune
Aptosimum lineare	carpet flower	river
Argemone subfusiformis	Mexican poppy/bloudissel (exotic)	river
Böophane disticha	poison bulb/gifbol	river and dune
Cassia italica	swartstorm	river
Citrullus lanatus	tsama	river and dune
Cleome gynandra	wild sweetpea/wilde-ertjie	dune
Cucumis africanus	wild cucumber	river
Crinum harmsii	vleilelie	river and dune
Elephantorrhiza elephantina	eland's wattle/elandsboontjie	dune
Geigeria ornativa	vermeerbos	river
G. pectidea	vermeerbos	river and dune
Gisekia africana	volstruisdruiwe	dune
G. pharnacioides	volstruisdruiwe	dune
Harpagophytum procumbens	devil's claw/kloudoring	dune
Helichrysum argyrosphaerum	sewejaartjie	river
Hermbstaedtia odorata	cat's tail/katstert	dune

Indigofera alternans	springbokopslag	river and dune
Nerine laticoma	vleilelie	river and dune
Oxygonum alatum	suring	dune
O. delagoense	suring	dune
Psoralea obtusifolia	rivierklawer	river
Sesamum triphyllum	brandboontjie	dune
Tribulus terrestris	duwweltjie	river and dune
T. zeyheri	duwweltjie	river

Perennial Grasses

Aristida meridionalis	rooisokkie	dune
Centropodia glauca	gha grass	dune
Eragrostis bicolor	speckled vlei grass/fynvleigras	river
E. lehmanniana	love grass/knietjiesgras	river and dune
E. pallens	gemsbok grass	dune
E. rotifer	vleipluimgras	river
Panicum coloratum	buffalo grass/buffelgras	river
Stipagrostis amabilis	dune reed/duinriet	dune
S. ciliata	tall bushman grass/ langbeenboesmangras	dune
S. obtusa	short bushman grass/ kortbeenboesmangras	river
S. uniplumis	silky bushman grass/ blinkhaargras	river and dune

Annual Grasses

Chloris virgata	feather top chloris/vleigras	river
Schmidtia kalahariensis	kalahari grass/suurgras	river and dune
Setaria verticillata	bristle burr grass/klitsgras	river

Additional reading

Barrow, B. 1975. *Song of a dry river*. Purnell, Cape Town.

Goldie, F. 1963. *Lost city of the Kalahari*. A.A. Balkema, Cape Town.

Green, L.G. 1948. *To the river's end*. Howard B. Timmins, Cape Town.

Kloppers, H. 1970. *Gee my 'n man!* Afrikaanse Pers-Boekhandel, Johannesburg.

Leistner, O.A. 1967. *The plant ecology of the southern Kalahari*. Mem. Bot. Survey of South Africa No 38. Government Printer, Pretoria.

Main, M. 1987. *Kalahari – Life's variety in dune and delta*. Southern Book Publishers, Johannesburg.

Mills, M.G.L. 1989. *Kalahari hyaenas: the comparative behavioural ecology of two species*. Unwin Hyman, London.

Proceedings of a symposium on the Kalahari held at Pretoria, October 1983. *Koedoe 27* (Supplement) 1984, National Parks Board, Pretoria.

Index